Earth's Surface

interactive SCIENCE

PEARSON

Boston, Massachusetts
Chandler, Arizona
Glenview, Illinois
Upper Saddle River, New Jersey

AUTHORS

You're an author!

As you write in this science book, your answers and personal discoveries will be recorded for you to keep, making this book unique to you. That is why you are one of the primary authors of this book.

✏️ **In the space below, print your name, school, town, and state. Then write a short autobiography that includes your interests and accomplishments.**

YOUR NAME _____

SCHOOL _____

TOWN, STATE _____

AUTOBIOGRAPHY _____

_____

_____

_____

_____

_____

_____

_____

Your Photo

Acknowledgments appear on pages 161–162, which constitutes an extension of this copyright page.

ISBN-13: 978-0-13-368485-8
ISBN-10: 0-13-368485-7

25 20

ON THE COVER
Geologic Formations
Delicate Arch is one of many geologic formations that visitors can explore at Utah's Arches National Park. The arches have formed over millions of years, but the forces of weathering and erosion continue to shape this dramatic landscape.

Program Authors

DON BUCKLEY, M.Sc.
Information and Communications Technology Director,
The School at Columbia University, New York, New York
Mr. Buckley has been at the forefront of K–12 educational technology for nearly two decades. A founder of New York City Independent School Technologists (NYCIST) and long-time chair of New York Association of Independent Schools' annual IT conference, he has taught students on two continents and created multimedia and Internet-based instructional systems for schools worldwide.

ZIPPORAH MILLER, M.A.Ed.
Associate Executive Director for Professional Programs
and Conferences, National Science Teachers Association,
Arlington, Virginia
Associate executive director for professional programs and conferences at NSTA, Ms. Zipporah Miller is a former K–12 science supervisor and STEM coordinator for the Prince George's County Public School District in Maryland. She is a science education consultant who has overseen curriculum development and staff training for more than 150 district science coordinators.

MICHAEL J. PADILLA, Ph.D.
Associate Dean and Director, Eugene P. Moore School of
Education, Clemson University, Clemson, South Carolina
A former middle school teacher and a leader in middle school science education, Dr. Michael Padilla has served as president of the National Science Teachers Association and as a writer of the National Science Education Standards. He is professor of science education at Clemson University. As lead author of the *Science Explorer* series, Dr. Padilla has inspired the team in developing a program that promotes student inquiry and meets the needs of today's students.

KATHRYN THORNTON, Ph.D.
Professor and Associate Dean, School of Engineering
and Applied Science, University of Virginia,
Charlottesville, Virginia
Selected by NASA in May 1984, Dr. Kathryn Thornton is a veteran of four space flights. She has logged over 975 hours in space, including more than 21 hours of extravehicular activity. As an author on the *Scott Foresman Science* series, Dr. Thornton's enthusiasm for science has inspired teachers around the globe.

MICHAEL E. WYSESSION, Ph.D.
Associate Professor of Earth and Planetary Science,
Washington University, St. Louis, Missouri
An author on more than 50 scientific publications, Dr. Wysession was awarded the prestigious Packard Foundation Fellowship and Presidential Faculty Fellowship for his research in geophysics. Dr. Wysession is an expert on Earth's inner structure and has mapped various regions of Earth using seismic tomography. He is known internationally for his work in geoscience education and outreach.

Instructional Design Author

GRANT WIGGINS, Ed.D.
President, Authentic Education,
Hopewell, New Jersey
Dr. Wiggins is a co-author with Jay McTighe of *Understanding by Design, 2nd Edition* (ASCD 2005). His approach to instructional design provides teachers with a disciplined way of thinking about curriculum design, assessment, and instruction that moves teaching from covering content to ensuring understanding.
UNDERSTANDING BY DESIGN® and UbD™ are trademarks of ASCD, and are used under license.

Planet Diary Author

JACK HANKIN
Science/Mathematics Teacher,
The Hilldale School, Daly City, California
Founder, Planet Diary Web site
Mr. Hankin is the creator and writer of Planet Diary, a science current events Web site. He is passionate about bringing science news and environmental awareness into classrooms and offers numerous Planet Diary workshops at NSTA and other events to train middle and high school teachers.

ELL Consultant

JIM CUMMINS, Ph.D.
Professor and Canada Research Chair,
Curriculum, Teaching and Learning
department at the University of Toronto
Dr. Cummins focuses on literacy development in multilingual schools and the role of technology in promoting student learning across the curriculum. *Interactive Science* incorporates essential research-based principles for integrating language with the teaching of academic content based on his instructional framework.

Reading Consultant

HARVEY DANIELS, Ph.D.
Professor of Secondary Education,
University of New Mexico,
Albuquerque, New Mexico
Dr. Daniels is an international consultant to schools, districts, and educational agencies. He has authored or coauthored 13 books on language, literacy, and education. His most recent works are *Comprehension and Collaboration: Inquiry Circles in Action* and *Subjects Matter: Every Teacher's Guide to Content-Area Reading.*

REVIEWERS

Contributing Writers

Edward Aguado, Ph.D.
Professor, Department of Geography
San Diego State University
San Diego, California

Elizabeth Coolidge-Stolz, M.D.
Medical Writer
North Reading, Massachusetts

Donald L. Cronkite, Ph.D.
Professor of Biology
Hope College
Holland, Michigan

Jan Jenner, Ph.D.
Science Writer
Talladega, Alabama

Linda Cronin Jones, Ph.D.
Associate Professor of Science and Environmental Education
University of Florida
Gainesville, Florida

T. Griffith Jones, Ph.D.
Clinical Associate Professor of Science Education
College of Education
University of Florida
Gainesville, Florida

Andrew C. Kemp, Ph.D.
Teacher
Jefferson County Public Schools
Louisville, Kentucky

Matthew Stoneking, Ph.D.
Associate Professor of Physics
Lawrence University
Appleton, Wisconsin

R. Bruce Ward, Ed.D.
Senior Research Associate
Science Education Department
Harvard-Smithsonian Center for Astrophysics
Cambridge, Massachusetts

Content Reviewers

Paul D. Beale, Ph.D.
Department of Physics
University of Colorado at Boulder
Boulder, Colorado

Jeff R. Bodart, Ph.D.
Professor of Physical Sciences
Chipola College
Marianna, Florida

Joy Branlund, Ph.D.
Department of Earth Science
Southwestern Illinois College
Granite City, Illinois

Marguerite Brickman, Ph.D.
Division of Biological Sciences
University of Georgia
Athens, Georgia

Bonnie J. Brunkhorst, Ph.D.
Science Education and Geological Sciences
California State University
San Bernardino, California

Michael Castellani, Ph.D.
Department of Chemistry
Marshall University
Huntington, West Virginia

Charles C. Curtis, Ph.D.
Research Associate Professor of Physics
University of Arizona
Tucson, Arizona

Diane I. Doser, Ph.D.
Department of Geological Sciences
University of Texas
El Paso, Texas

Rick Duhrkopf, Ph.D.
Department of Biology
Baylor University
Waco, Texas

Alice K. Hankla, Ph.D.
The Galloway School
Atlanta, Georgia

Mark Henriksen, Ph.D.
Physics Department
University of Maryland
Baltimore, Maryland

Chad Hershock, Ph.D.
Center for Research on Learning and Teaching
University of Michigan
Ann Arbor, Michigan

Jeremiah N. Jarrett, Ph.D.
Department of Biology
Central Connecticut State University
New Britain, Connecticut

Scott L. Kight, Ph.D.
Department of Biology
Montclair State University
Montclair, New Jersey

Jennifer O. Liang, Ph.D.
Department of Biology
University of Minnesota–Duluth
Duluth, Minnesota

Candace Lutzow-Felling, Ph.D.
Director of Education
The State Arboretum of Virginia
University of Virginia
Boyce, Virginia

Cortney V. Martin, Ph.D.
Virginia Polytechnic Institute
Blacksburg, Virginia

Joseph F. McCullough, Ph.D.
Physics Program Chair
Cabrillo College
Aptos, California

Heather Mernitz, Ph.D.
Department of Physical Science
Alverno College
Milwaukee, Wisconsin

Sadredin C. Moosavi, Ph.D.
Department of Earth and Environmental Sciences
Tulane University
New Orleans, Louisiana

David L. Reid, Ph.D.
Department of Biology
Blackburn College
Carlinville, Illinois

Scott M. Rochette, Ph.D.
Department of the Earth Sciences
SUNY College at Brockport
Brockport, New York

Karyn L. Rogers, Ph.D.
Department of Geological Sciences
University of Missouri
Columbia, Missouri

Laurence Rosenhein, Ph.D.
Department of Chemistry
Indiana State University
Terre Haute, Indiana

Sara Seager, Ph.D.
Department of Planetary Sciences and Physics
Massachusetts Institute of Technology
Cambridge, Massachusetts

Tom Shoberg, Ph.D.
Missouri University of Science and Technology
Rolla, Missouri

Patricia Simmons, Ph.D.
North Carolina State University
Raleigh, North Carolina

William H. Steinecker, Ph.D.
Research Scholar
Miami University
Oxford, Ohio

Paul R. Stoddard, Ph.D.
Department of Geology and Environmental Geosciences
Northern Illinois University
DeKalb, Illinois

John R. Villarreal, Ph.D.
Department of Chemistry
The University of Texas–Pan American
Edinburg, Texas

John R. Wagner, Ph.D.
Department of Geology
Clemson University
Clemson, South Carolina

Jerry Waldvogel, Ph.D.
Department of Biological Sciences
Clemson University
Clemson, South Carolina

Donna L. Witter, Ph.D.
Department of Geology
Kent State University
Kent, Ohio

Edward J. Zalisko, Ph.D.
Department of Biology
Blackburn College
Carlinville, Illinois

Museum of Science

Special thanks to the Museum of Science, Boston, Massachusetts, and Ioannis Miaoulis, the Museum's president and director, for serving as content advisors for the technology and design strand in this program.

CONTENTS

 **Enter the Lab zone for hands-on inquiry.**

Chapter Lab Investigation:
• Directed Inquiry: A Map in a Pan
• Open Inquiry: A Map in a Pan

Inquiry Warm-Ups: • What Is the Land Like Around Your School? • How Can You Flatten the Curved Earth? • Make a Pixel Picture • Can a Map Show Relief?

Quick Labs: • Surface Features • Modeling Landforms • 2-D and 3-D Maps • Measuring in Degrees • Where in the World? • Reading Satellite Images • Where Are You?

my science online.com

Go to MyScienceOnline.com to interact with this chapter's content.
Keyword: Mapping Earth's Surface

> UNTAMED SCIENCE
• Extreme Mapping

> PLANET DIARY
• Mapping Earth's Surface

> INTERACTIVE ART
• Make a Map • Topographic Maps

> ART IN MOTION
• Global Positioning System (GPS)

> REAL-WORLD INQUIRY
• Placing a Bay Area Stadium

Lab zone® **Enter the Lab zone for hands-on inquiry.**

Chapter Lab Investigation:
• Directed Inquiry: Investigating Soils and Drainage
• Open Inquiry: Investigating Soils and Drainage

Inquiry Warm-Ups: • How Fast Can It Fizz? • What Is Soil? • How Can You Keep Soil From Washing Away?

Quick Labs: • Freezing and Thawing • Rusting Away • It's All on the Surface • The Contents of Soil • Using It Up • Soil Conservation

my science online.com

Go to MyScienceOnline.com to interact with this chapter's content. Keyword: Weathering and Soil

> **UNTAMED SCIENCE**
• Tafoni, No Bologna

> **PLANET DIARY**
• Weathering and Soil

> **INTERACTIVE ART**
• The Forces of Weathering • Soil Layers

> **ART IN MOTION**
• Mechanical and Chemical Weathering

> **REAL-WORLD INQUIRY**
• Being Smart About Soil

CONTENTS

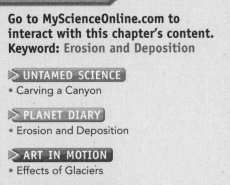

Enter the Lab zone for hands-on inquiry.

Chapter Lab Investigation:
• Directed Inquiry: Sand Hills
• Open Inquiry: Sand Hills

Inquiry Warm-Ups: • How Does Gravity Affect Materials on a Slope? • How Does Moving Water Wear Away Rocks? • How Do Glaciers Change the Land? • What Is Sand Made Of? • How Does Moving Air Affect Sediment?

Quick Labs: • Weathering and Erosion • Raindrops Falling • Erosion Cube • Surging Glaciers • Modeling Valleys • Shaping a Coastline • Desert Pavement

my science online.com

Go to MyScienceOnline.com to interact with this chapter's content. Keyword: **Erosion and Deposition**

UNTAMED SCIENCE
• Carving a Canyon

PLANET DIARY
• Erosion and Deposition

ART IN MOTION
• Effects of Glaciers

INTERACTIVE ART
• Effects of Waves • Mass Movement

REAL-WORLD INQUIRY
• Why Live Where It Floods?

Lab® zone Enter the Lab zone for hands-on inquiry.

Chapter Lab Investigation:
• Directed Inquiry: Exploring Geologic Time Through Core Samples
• Open Inquiry: Exploring Geologic Time Through Core Samples

Inquiry Warm-Ups: • What's in a Rock? • Which Layer Is the Oldest? • How Long Till It's Gone? • This Is Your Life! • How Could Planet Earth Form in Space? • Dividing History

Quick Labs: • Sweet Fossils • Modeling Trace Fossils • Modeling the Fossil Record • How Did It Form? • The Dating Game • How Old Is It? • Going Back in Time • Learning From Fossils • Graphing the Fossil Record • Modeling an Asteroid Impact • Cenozoic Timeline

my science online.com

Go to MyScienceOnline.com to interact with this chapter's content.
Keyword: A Trip Through Geologic Time

> **PLANET DIARY**
• A Trip Through Geologic Time

> **ART IN MOTION**
• Change Over Geologic Time

> **INTERACTIVE ART**
• Piecing Together the Past • Index Fossils
• Fossil Formation

> **REAL-WORLD INQUIRY**
• How Do You Find the Age of a Rock?

interactive SCIENCE

This is your book.
You can write in it!

THE BIG
?Q

Get Engaged!

At the start of each chapter, you will see two questions: an Engaging Question and the Big Question. Each chapter's Big Question will help you start thinking about the Big Ideas of Science. Look for the Big Q symbol throughout the chapter!

HOW CAN **WIND** KEEP YOUR **LIGHTS ON?**

?THE BIG
What are some of Earth's energy sources?

This man is repairing a wind turbine at a wind farm in Texas. Most wind turbines are at least 30 meters off the ground where the winds are fast. Wind speed and blade length help determine the best way to capture the wind and turn it into power. Develop Hypotheses Why do you think people are working to increase the amount of power we get from wind?

Wind energy collected by the
turbine does not cause air pollution.

UNTAMED SCIENCE Watch the **Untamed Science** video to learn more about energy resources.

174 Energy Resources

Untamed Science

Follow the Untamed Science video crew as they travel the globe exploring the Big Ideas of Science.

Interact with your textbook.　　Interact with inquiry.　　Interact online.

Energy Resources

CHAPTER
5

Build Reading, Inquiry, and Vocabulary Skills

In every lesson you will learn new ↺ Reading and ▲ Inquiry skills. These skills will help you read and think like a scientist. Vocabulary skills will help you communicate effectively and uncover the meaning of words.

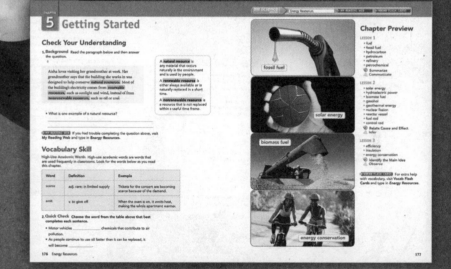

Go Online!

Look for the MyScienceOnline.com technology options. At MyScienceOnline.com you can immerse yourself in amazing virtual environments, get extra practice, and even blog about current events in science.

Explore the Key Concepts.

Each lesson begins with a series of Key Concept questions. The interactivities in each lesson will help you understand these concepts and Unlock the Big Question.

MY PLANET DIARY

At the start of each lesson, My Planet Diary will introduce you to amazing events, significant people, and important discoveries in science or help you to overcome common misconceptions about science concepts.

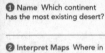

Explain what you know.

Look for the pencil. When you see it, it's time to interact with your book and demonstrate what you have learned.

Elaborate further with the Apply It activities. This is your opportunity to take what you've learned and apply those skills to new situations.

Lab Zone

Look for the Lab zone triangle. This means it's time to do a hands-on inquiry lab. In every lesson, you'll have the opportunity to do a hands-on inquiry activity that will help reinforce your understanding of the lesson topic.

ile area becomes depleted come a desert. The s that previously were h fih KAY shun). For example, a **drought** s in an area. During the exposed soil easily cattle and sheep and desertification, too. eople cannot grow crops has occurred. As a result, esertification is severe in ere are moving to the themselves on the land.

areas where there n the map to support

cation, what are some s effects?

Land Reclamation Fortunately, it is possible to replace land damaged by erosion or mining. The process of restoring an area of land to a more productive state is called **land reclamation.** In addition to restoring land for agriculture, land reclamation can restore habitats for wildlife. Many different types of land reclamation projects are currently underway all over the world. But it is generally more difficult and expensive to restore damaged land and soil than it is to protect those resources in the first place. In some cases, the land may not return to its original state.

FIGURE 4

Land Reclamation

These pictures show land before and after it was mined.

Communicate Below the pictures, write a story about what happened to the land.

Do the Quick Lab *Modeling S*

Assess Your Understanding

1a. Review Subsoil has (less/more) plant and animal matter than topsoil.

b. Explain What can happen to soil if plants are removed?

c. Apply Concepts that could pre land reclam

got it?

O I get it! Now I know that soil management is important beca

O I need extra help with

Go to MY SCIENCE COACH online for help with this subject.

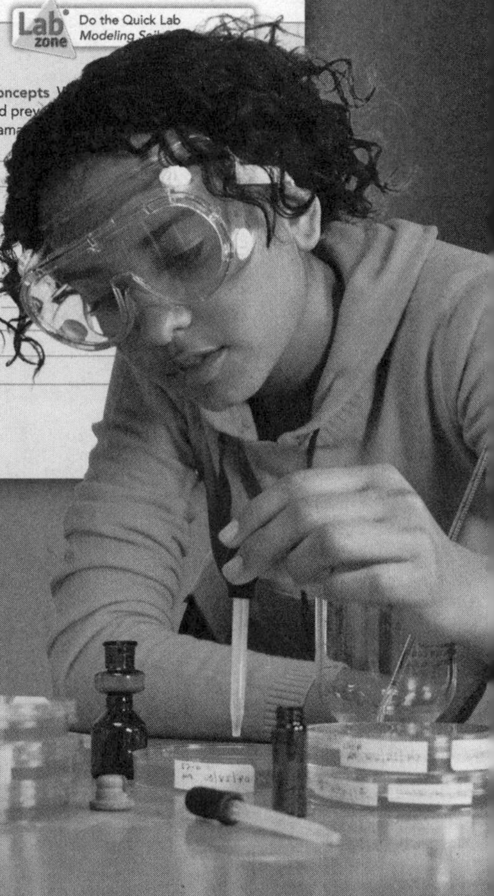

got it?

Evaluate Your Progress.

After answering the Got It question, think about how you're doing. Did you get it or do you need a little help? Remember, MY SCIENCE COACH is there for you if you need extra help.

Explore the Big Question.

At one point in the chapter, you'll have the opportunity to take all that you've learned to further explore the Big Question.

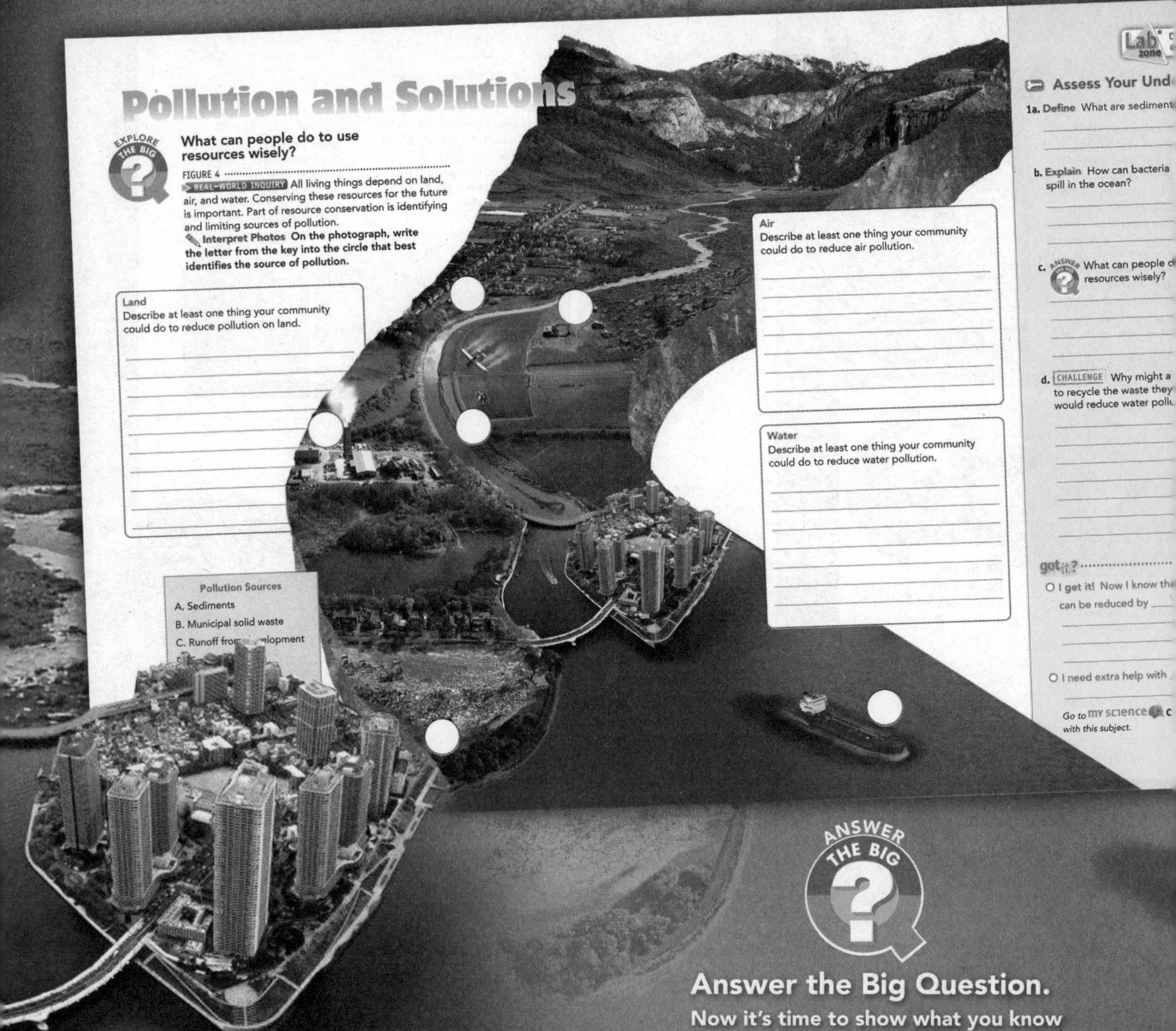

Pollution and Solutions

What can people do to use resources wisely?

FIGURE 4 ....

> REAL-WORLD INQUIRY All living things depend on land, air, and water. Conserving these resources for the future is important. Part of resource conservation is identifying and limiting sources of pollution.

✎ **Interpret Photos** On the photograph, write the letter from the key into the circle that best identifies the source of pollution.

Land
Describe at least one thing your community could do to reduce pollution on land.

_____

_____

_____

_____

Air
Describe at least one thing your community could do to reduce air pollution.

_____

_____

_____

Water
Describe at least one thing your community could do to reduce water pollution.

_____

_____

_____

Pollution Sources

A. Sediments

B. Municipal solid waste

C. Runoff from development

Lab zone

▭ **Assess Your Und**

1a. Define What are sediment

_____

b. Explain How can bacteria
spill in the ocean?

_____

c. ANSWER What can people d
resources wisely?

_____

d. CHALLENGE Why might a
to recycle the waste they
would reduce water pollu

_____

_____

_____

_____

got it? ....

○ I get it! Now I know th
can be reduced by ____

○ I need extra help with

Go to MY SCIENCE ▨ c
with this subject.

Answer the Big Question.

Now it's time to show what you know and answer the Big Question.

Review What You've Learned.

Use the Chapter Study Guide to review the Big Question and prepare for the test.

CHAPTER 4 Study Guide

To use resources wisely, people can reuse or _____ materials and they can properly dispose of hazardous wastes and other _____.

LESSON 1 Conserving Land and Soil

Three uses that change the land are agriculture, mining, and development.

Without soil, most life on land could not exist. Poor soil management results in three problems: erosion, nutrient depletion, and desertification.

Vocabulary
• litter • topsoil • subsoil • bedrock
• erosion • nutrient depletion • fertilizer
• desertification • drought • land reclamation

LESSON 2 Waste Disposal and Recycling

Solid waste is burned, buried, or recycled.

Recycling categories include metal, glass, paper, and plastic.

Hazardous wastes are stored depending on the type and potential danger.

Vocabulary
• municipal solid waste • incineration
• pollutant • leachate • sanitary landfill
• recycling • biodegradable • hazardous waste

LESSON 3 Air Pollution and Solutions

A major source of outdoor air pollution is vehicle emissions. Indoor air pollution has a variety of causes.

The major cause of the ozone hole is CFCs.

Reducing air pollution requires reducing emissions.

Vocabulary
• emissions • photochemical smog • ozone
• temperature inversion • acid rain
• radon • ozone layer • chlorofluorocarbon

LESSON 4 Water Pollution and Solutions

Water on Earth is about 97 percent saltwater.

Most water pollution is caused by human activities.

The keys to keeping water clean include cleaning oil spills, proper sewage treatment, and the reduction of pollutants.

Vocabulary
• groundwater • pesticide • sewage • sediment

LESSON 5 Ocean Resources

Resources in the ocean include organisms such as fish and nonliving things such as oil.

Most ocean pollution is related to human activities.

Vocabulary
• nodule
• upwelling

168 Land, Air, and Water Resources

Review and Assessment

LESSON 1 Conserving Land and Soil

1. What is an agricultural use of land?
   a. growing crops on land
   b. collecting water from land
   c. building structures on land
   d. removing minerals from land

2. Plant roots absorb nutrients and water from the layer of soil called _____.

3. Relate Cause and Effect What type of land use can result in nutrient depletion? Explain.

LESSON 3 Air Pollution and Solutions

7. Which of the following describes a pollutant that has been released into the air?
   a. sewage   b. leachate
   c. sediment   d. emissions

8. The _____ in the upper atmosphere prevents some of the sun's ultraviolet radiation from reaching Earth.

9. Predict Do you think the hole in the ozone layer will increase or decrease in size? Why?

CHAPTER 4 Review and Assessment

LESSON 4 Water Pollution and Solutions

11. Why is fresh water a limited resource?
    a. because most water on Earth is in lakes
    b. because most water on Earth is in clouds
    c. because most water on Earth is in the ground
    d. because most water on Earth is salt water

12. A _____ is a chemical that kills crop-destroying organisms.

13. Draw Conclusions Rain may wash fertilizers into bodies of water, such as ponds. How might fertilizer affect a pond?

What can people do to use resources wisely?

17. Every individual, including young people, can make decisions to use resources wisely. Use the terms reduce, reuse, and recycle to explain how the students in the picture below can help minimize solid waste.

LESSON 5 Ocean Resources

14. The ocean contains living resources such as _____ and nonliving resources such as _____.
    a. fuel; water   b. fish; minerals
    c. seaweed; shrimp   d. organisms; pollution

15. _____ is the movement of cold water from the deep ocean to the surface.

16. Relate Cause and Effect How might oil used as fuel result in ocean pollution?

170 Land, Air, and Water Resources

159

Practice Taking Tests.

Apply the Big Question and take a practice test in standardized test format.

Go to **MyScienceOnline.com** and immerse yourself in amazing virtual environments.

▷ THE BIG QUESTION

Each online chapter starts with a Big Question. Your mission is to unlock the meaning of this Big Question as each science lesson unfolds.

▷ VOCAB FLASH CARDS

Practice chapter vocabulary with interactive flash cards. Each card has an image, definitions in English and Spanish, and space for your own notes.

▷ INTERACTIVE ART

At MyScienceOnline.com, many of the beautiful visuals in your book become interactive so you can extend your learning.

WITH INQUIRY...

interactive SCIENCE
GO ONLINE

my science online.com ▶ Populations and Communities ▷ PLANET DIARY ▷ LAB ZONE ▷ VIRTUAL LAB

↻ ＋ 🌐 http://www.myscienceonline.com/

▷ PLANET DIARY

My Planet Diary online is the place to find more information and activities related to the topic in the lesson.

[window]

Elaborate | Evaluate

t Everest

Tools
123

Still Growing! Mount Everest in the Himalayas is the highest mountain on Earth. Climbers who reach the peak stand 8,850 meters above sea level. You might think that mountains never change. But forces inside Earth push Mount Everest at least several millimeters higher each year. Over time, Earth's forces slowly but constantly lift, stretch, bend, and break Earth's crust in dramatic ways!

▷ Planet Diary Go to Planet Diary to learn more about forces in the Earth's crust.

Next
22 of 22
Back

[window]

Elaborate | Evaluate

Tools
123

0:35 / 1:30

Next
22 of 22
Back

▷ VIRTUAL LAB

Get more practice with realistic virtual labs. Manipulate the variables on-screen and test your hypothesis.

Find Your Chapter

1 Go to www.myscienceonline.com.

2 Log in with username and password.

3 Click on your program and select your chapter.

Keyword Search

1 Go to www.myscienceonline.com.

2 Log in with username and password.

3 Click on your program and select Search.

4 Enter the keyword (from your book) in the search box.

Other Content Available Online

▷ **UNTAMED SCIENCE** Follow these young scientists through their amazing online video blogs as they travel the globe in search of answers to the Big Questions of Science.

▷ **MY SCIENCE COACH** Need extra help? My Science Coach is your personal online study partner. My Science Coach is a chance for you to get more practice on key science concepts. There you can choose from a variety of tools that will help guide you through each science lesson.

▷ **MY READING WEB** Need extra reading help on a particular science topic? At My Reading Web you will find a choice of reading selections targeted to your specific reading level.

Have you ever worked on a jigsaw puzzle? Usually a puzzle has a theme that leads you to group the pieces by what they have in common. But until you put all the pieces together you can't solve the puzzle. Studying science is similar to solving a puzzle. The big ideas of science are like puzzle themes. To understand big ideas, scientists ask questions. The answers to those questions are like pieces of a puzzle. Each chapter in this book asks a big question to help you think about a big idea of science. By answering the big questions, you will get closer to understanding the big idea.

✎ **Before you read each chapter, write about what you know and what more you'd like to know.**

BIGIDEA
Earth is a continually changing planet.

Desert winds can pile up giant sand dunes.

What do you already know about changes on Earth? ✎ **What more would you like to know?**

_____

_____

Big Question:

❓ How is a map a model of Earth? Chapter 1

❓ What processes break down rock? Chapter 2

❓ What processes shape the surface of the land? Chapter 3

✎ **After reading the chapters, write what you have learned about the Big Idea.**

_____

_____

Over millions of years, the Colorado River cut through layers of solid rock to form the Grand Canyon in Arizona.

Earth is 4.6 billion years old and the rock record contains its history.

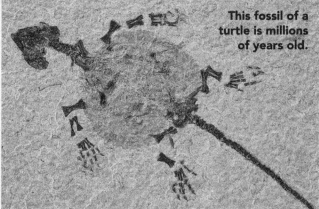

This fossil of a turtle is millions of years old.

What do you already know about Earth's history?
✏️ **What more would you like to know?**

_____

_____

_____

Big Question:

❓ How do scientists study Earth's past?
Chapter 4

✏️ **After reading the chapter, write what you have learned about the Big Idea.**

_____

_____

_____

HOW WILL THIS CLIMBER FIND HIS WAY HOME?

THE BIG ? How is a map a model of Earth?

Somewhere far from home or hotels, in the middle of a long climb, a hiker needs somewhere to sleep. This climber set up his tent on the face of a cliff in Yosemite National Park. He will rest and have his dinner in this hanging tent called a portaledge. When he wakes up the next morning and finishes his climb, which trail will he take to get down? ✎ **Infer** **How might you find your way home from a hike in the mountains?**

_____

_____

_____

_____

_____

_____

> UNTAMED SCIENCE Watch the **Untamed Science** video to learn more about maps.

Mapping Earth's Surface

1 Getting Started

Check Your Understanding

1. **Background** Read the paragraph below and then answer the question.

> Dr. Lyndon collected **data** for her research study on North American plants. First, she looked at how plants grow in each **region.** She recorded what local crops were sold in the cities of that region. Then she compared different regions on the **continent** of North America.

> **Data** are pieces of information, often in the form of facts or figures, usually collected for study.
>
> A **region** is an area of land sharing one or more characteristics.
>
> A **continent** is any one of seven large landmasses on Earth.

- What data helped Dr. Lyndon compare plant growth?

_____

_____

> **MY READING WEB** If you had trouble completing the question above, visit **My Reading Web** and type in *Mapping Earth's Surface.*

Vocabulary Skill

Identify Multiple Meanings In science, it is important to use terms precisely. Some familiar words have more than one meaning. Words you use every day may have different meanings in science. Look at the different meanings of the words below.

Word	Everyday Meaning	Scientific Meaning
key	*n.* Tool for locking and unlocking	*n.* List of symbols on a map, along with their explanations
degree	*n.* A relative amount of something	*n.* Unit for measuring distance around a circle, such as in longitude and latitude

2. **Quick Check** Circle the sentence below that uses the scientific meaning of the word *key.*

- Nick couldn't open the door without his key.
- The key shows that a picture of a tree stands for forest lands.

mountain

globe

aerial photograph

topographic map

Allen Mountain

Chapter Preview

LESSON 1
- topography • elevation
- relief • landform • plain
- mountain • mountain range
- plateau • landform region

↻ **Sequence**
△ **Classify**

LESSON 2
- globe • map
- map projection • symbol
- key • scale • degree
- equator • hemisphere
- prime meridian • latitude
- longitude

↻ **Identify the Main Idea**
△ **Measure**

LESSON 3
- surveying • digitizing
- pixel • aerial photograph
- satellite image
- Global Positioning System
- Geographic Information System

↻ **Relate Text and Visuals**
△ **Make Models**

LESSON 4
- topographic map
- contour line
- contour interval
- index contour

↻ **Compare and Contrast**
△ **Make Models**

▶ VOCAB FLASH CARDS For extra help with vocabulary, visit **Vocab Flash Cards** and type in *Mapping Earth's Surface.*

3

Exploring Earth's Surface

UNLOCK THE BIG ?

🔑 **What Does the Topography of an Area Include?**

🔑 **What Are the Main Types of Landforms?**

my pLaneT DiaRY

Lewis and Clark

In 1804, an expedition set out from near St. Louis to explore the land between the Mississippi River and the Pacific Ocean. The United States had just purchased a part of this vast territory from France. Few had traveled far to the west.

Led by Meriwether Lewis and William Clark, the expedition first traveled up the Missouri River. Then the group crossed the Rocky Mountains and followed the Columbia River to the Pacific Ocean.

DISCOVERY

If you were going on an expedition to explore unknown territory, what supplies would you bring with you?

_____

_____

_____

▶ PLANET DIARY Go to **Planet Diary** to learn more about landforms and topography.

 Lab zone® Do the Inquiry Warm-Up *What Is the Land Like Around Your School?*

What Does the Topography of an Area Include?

On the journey to the Pacific, the Lewis and Clark expedition traveled more than 5,000 kilometers. As they traveled, Lewis and Clark observed many changes in topography. **Topography** (tuh PAWG ruh fee) is the shape of the land. An area's topography may be flat, sloping, hilly, or mountainous. 🔑 **The topography of an area includes the area's elevation, relief, and landforms.**

Elevation The height above sea level of a point on Earth's surface is its **elevation.** When Lewis and Clark started their expedition, they were about 140 meters above sea level. By the time they reached Lemhi Pass in the Rocky Mountains, they were more than 2,200 meters above sea level. Look at **Figure 1** to see the changes in elevation along Lewis and Clark's route.

Vocabulary

- topography • elevation • relief • landform
- plain • mountain • mountain range • plateau
- landform region

Skills

↻ Reading: Sequence

△ Inquiry: Classify

Relief The difference in elevation between the highest and lowest parts of an area is its **relief**. Early in their journey, Lewis and Clark encountered flat or rolling land that had low relief, or small differences in elevation. In the Rocky Mountains, they crossed huge mountains separated by deep valleys. These areas had high relief, or great differences in elevation.

Landforms If you followed the route of the Lewis and Clark expedition, you would see many different landforms. A **landform** is a feature of topography, such as a hill or valley, formed by the processes that shape Earth's surface. Different landforms have different combinations of elevation and relief.

FIGURE 1 ·······················

Lewis & Clark's Journey
The route of the Lewis and Clark expedition crossed regions that differed greatly in elevation and relief. ✎ **Calculate** Circle the highest and lowest points on their route. What is the relief between these two points?

_____

_____

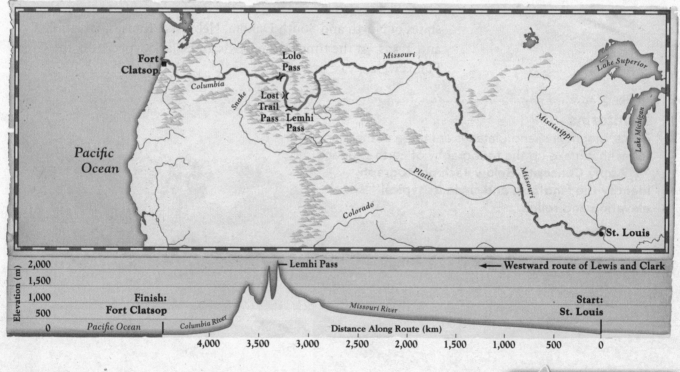

Do the Quick Lab
Surface Features.

🔑 Assess Your Understanding

got it? ··

- ○ I get it! Now I know topography of an area includes _____
- ○ I need extra help with _____

Go to **my science** **COACH** online for help with this subject.

What Are the Main Types of Landforms?

Landforms vary greatly in size and shape. They include level plains extending as far as the eye can see, rounded hills that you could climb on foot, and jagged mountains difficult to hike through. 🔑 **Three major types of landforms are plains, mountains, and plateaus.**

Plains

A **plain** is a landform made up of nearly flat or gently rolling land with low relief. A plain that lies along a seacoast is called a coastal plain. In North America, a coastal plain extends around the continent's eastern and southeastern shores. Coastal plains have both low elevation and low relief.

A plain that lies away from the coast is called an interior plain. Interior plains are often low and have low relief, but their elevations can vary. The broad interior plains of North America are called the Great Plains.

The Great Plains extend north from Texas into Canada. The Great Plains also extend west to the Rocky Mountains from the states of North and South Dakota, Nebraska, Kansas, Oklahoma, and Texas. At the time of the Lewis and Clark expedition, the Great Plains were a vast grassland.

FIGURE 2 ....

Landforms

Plains, mountains, and plateaus are three of the many landforms that make up the topography of Earth's surface.

✏️ **Apply Concepts** Below each photograph, identify the landform and circle its typical elevation and relief.

Landform: _____

Elevation: High / Low

Relief: High / Low

Mountains A **mountain** is a landform with high elevation and high relief. A mountain's base can cover an area of several square kilometers or more. Mountains usually exist as part of a mountain range. A **mountain range** is a group of mountains that are closely related in shape, structure, area, and age. After crossing the Great Plains, the Lewis and Clark expedition crossed a rugged mountain range in Idaho called the Bitterroot Mountains.

The different mountain ranges in a region make up a mountain system. The Bitterroot Mountains are one mountain range in the mountain system known as the Rocky Mountains.

Mountain ranges and mountain systems in a long, connected chain form a larger unit called a mountain belt. The Rocky Mountains are part of a great mountain belt that stretches down the western sides of North America and South America.

Plateaus A landform that has high elevation and a more or less level surface is called a **plateau.** A plateau is rarely perfectly smooth on top. Streams and rivers may cut into the plateau's surface. The Columbia Plateau in Washington State is an example. The Columbia River, which the Lewis and Clark expedition followed, slices through this plateau. The many layers of rock that make up the Columbia Plateau rise as high as 1,500 meters.

✎ **Sequence** Place these features in order from smallest to largest: mountain system, mountain range, mountain belt, mountain.

_____

_____

_____

_____

Landform: _____

Elevation: High / Low

Relief: High / Low

Landform: _____

Elevation: High / Low

Relief: High / Low

Landform Regions

A large area of land where the topography is made up mainly of one type of landform is called a **landform region.** The Great Plains and the Rocky Mountains are examples of major landform regions, as are the Great Basin, the Colorado Plateau, the Sierra Nevada Coastal Range, and the Atlantic Coastal Plain. All of the land in one major landform region tends to have much in common. For example, the land of the Atlantic Coastal Plain is generally of low elevation and relief. The plain forms an apron of rocky material that slopes gently down from the Appalachian Mountains to the ocean. The Great Basin is mostly desert land at high elevation. Much of the Great Basin is made up of broad valleys separated by mountain ranges.

Other terms can be used to describe landform regions. For example, an upland is a region of hilly topography. The Superior Uplands, located near Lake Superior, include hilly terrain. A lowland is a region of plains with low elevation. The Central Lowlands are an area of plains bordered by areas of higher elevation.

did you know?

The highest elevation in the United States is Mt. McKinley, Alaska, at 6,194 meters. The lowest is Death Valley, California, at 86 meters below sea level.

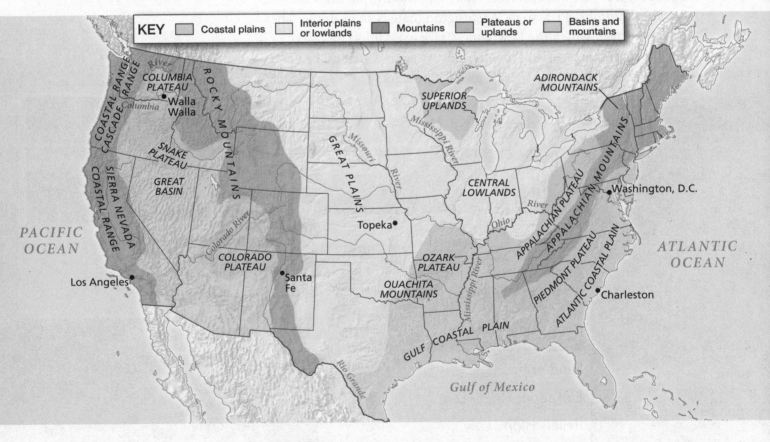

FIGURE 3

Landform Regions of the United States

The United States has many different landform regions.

✏️ Classify **Circle your home state (or another state) on the map and classify it by landform region(s).**

apply it!

Use the picture to answer the questions.

1 Use words to describe the topography shown in the picture.

_____

_____

2 Classify Classify the picture by the type of landform region.

_____

Rocky Mountains

Colorado Plateau

Great Plains

Lab zone® Do the Quick Lab *Modeling Landforms.*

🔑 Assess Your Understanding

1a. List What are the three main types of landforms?

_____

_____

b. Compare and Contrast How are plateaus and mountains alike? How are they different?

_____

_____

_____

c. Apply Concepts Which landform would be hardest to hike through? Why?

_____

_____

_____

got it?......................................

○ **I get it!** Now I know that the main types

of landforms are _____

_____

○ I need extra help with _____

Go to MY SCIENCE COACH online for help with this subject.

Models of Earth

UNLOCK THE BIG ?

🔑 How Do Maps and Globes Represent Earth?

🔑 How Is Distance Measured in Degrees?

🔑 What Are Latitude and Longitude?

my planeT DiaRY

DISCOVERY

Measuring Earth

Around 240 B.C., near the day of the summer solstice, the Greek scientist Eratosthenes (276–194 B.C.) calculated Earth's size. On that day, the sun was directly overhead at noon when viewed from the city of Syene, and its image was reflected in a well. At the same moment in Alexandria, to the north, the sun was not directly overhead. Instead, it appeared about $\frac{1}{50}$ of a circle south of the point directly overhead. Eratosthenes reasoned that the distance between the cities would be about $\frac{1}{50}$ of the distance around Earth. He multiplied the distance between the cities by 50 and found that Earth's circumference was 39,400 kilometers. This figure is very close to the modern measurement of 40,075 kilometers.

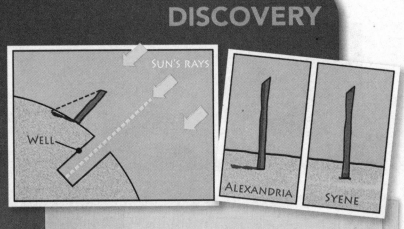

SUN'S RAYS

WELL

ALEXANDRIA   SYENE

✏️ **Communicate** Write your answer to each question below. Then discuss your answers with a partner.

1. What science skills did Eratosthenes use when he estimated Earth's circumference?

_____

_____

2. On the summer solstice, would a stick cast a shadow where you live? Why or why not?

_____

_____

_____

▶ PLANET DIARY Go to **Planet Diary** to learn more about reading maps.

Lab® zone   Do the Inquiry Warm-Up *How Can You Flatten the Curved Earth?*

Vocabulary

- globe   - map   - map projection   - symbol
- key   - scale   - degree   - equator   - hemisphere
- prime meridian   - latitude   - longitude

Skills

↻ **Reading:** Identify the Main Idea

△ **Inquiry:** Measure

How Do Maps and Globes Represent Earth?

Maps and globes show the shape, size, and position of features on Earth's surface. A **globe** is a sphere that represents Earth's entire surface. A **map** is a flat model of all or part of Earth's surface as seen from above. **Maps and globes are drawn to scale and use symbols to represent features on Earth's surface. To show Earth's curved surface on a flat map, mapmakers use map projections.**

Map Projection A **map projection** is a framework of lines that helps to transfer points on Earth's three-dimensional surface onto a flat map. Continents, oceans, islands, rivers, and lakes might appear to have somewhat different sizes and shapes due to the map projection used. A Mercator projection is just one of many projections that allow mapmakers to show a curved Earth on a flat surface. On a Mercator projection, the size and shape of landmasses become more and more distorted toward the north and south poles.

Vocabulary Use Context to Determine Meaning Show you understand the word *model* by explaining how a globe is a model of Earth.

_____

_____

_____

_____

_____

FIGURE 1 ·······································

Mercator Projection

A Mercator projection is based on a cylinder with grid lines that has been flattened.

✎ **Interpret Maps** Look at the landmasses on both the globe and the map. How are the images alike and how are they different on the two maps?

_____

_____

_____

_____

_____

_____

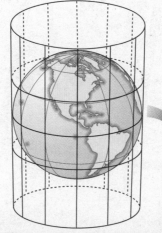

FIGURE 2 ·················

INTERACTIVE ART **What's in a Map?**
A map is drawn to scale, uses symbols explained in a key, and usually has a compass rose to show direction.

WELCOME TO
Central City

Symbols and Key

Mapmakers use shapes and pictures called **symbols** to stand for features on Earth's surface. A symbol can represent a physical feature, such as a river, lake, mountain, or plain. A symbol can also stand for a human-made feature, such as a highway, city, or airport. A map's **key,** or legend, is a list of all the symbols used on the map, with an explanation of their meanings. Maps also include a compass rose or north arrow. The compass rose helps relate directions on the map to directions on Earth's surface. North usually is located at the top of the map.

Key

- 🏫 **School**
- ❓ **Tourist information**
- Ⓗ **Hospital**
- 🍴 **Restaurant**
- 🛍️ **Shopping center**
- – – **Cycle route**

Elm Park

Market Plaza

Main Street

First Street
Second Street
Third Street
Fourth Street
Fifth Street

Map Scale

Ratio scale 1 : 2,500

Bar scale

| 0 | 100 | 200 | 300 ft |
| 0 | 25 | 50 | 75 | 100 m |

Equivalent units scale
1 cm = 25 m

Scale

A map's **scale** relates distance on a map to distance on Earth's surface. Scale is often given as a ratio. For example, one unit on a map could equal 2,500 units on the ground. So 1 centimeter on the map would represent 2,500 centimeters, or 25 meters. This scale, "one to two thousand five hundred," would be written as the ratio "1 : 2,500." **Figure 2** shows three ways of giving a map's scale.

✏️ **Identify the Main Idea** How do mapmakers relate distance on a map to distances on Earth's surface?

_____

_____

do the math! Sample Problem

Scale and Ratios

A ratio compares two numbers by division. For example, the scale of a particular map is given as a ratio of 1 : 250,000. At this scale, the distance between two points on the map measures 23.5 cm. How would you find the actual distance?

STEP 1 **Write the scale as a fraction.**

$$\frac{1}{250,000}$$

STEP 2 Write a proportion. Let d represent the distance between the two points.

$$\frac{1}{250,000} = \frac{23.5 \text{ cm}}{d}$$

STEP 3 Write the cross products. (*Hint:* To convert cm to km, divide d by 100,000.)

$$1 \times d = 250,000 \times 23.5 \text{ cm}$$

$$d = 5,875,000 \text{ cm, or } 58.75 \text{ km}$$

· Practice! ·

Use the formula in the sample problem to solve the problem below.

Calculate A map's scale is 1 : 25,000. If two points are 4.7 cm apart on the map, how far apart are they on the ground?

✎ **Answer the following questions.**

1. What is the scale of this map in equivalent units?

_____

2. Circle all the locations on the map where you can buy food.

3. Create a symbol for a gas station and draw it at the southwest corner of Fourth St. and Main St. The distance on the map between the school and the gas station is about 6 cm. According to the scale, how far is that distance on Earth's surface?

_____

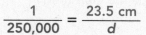 Do the Quick Lab 2-D and 3-D Maps.

🔑 Assess Your Understanding

1a. Describe A (symbol/key) is a picture that stands for a feature on Earth's surface.

b. Summarize What are some physical features that can be shown on a map?

_____

_____

_____

_____

**got it? ** ·

○ **I get it!** Now I know that maps and globes are

_____

_____

○ **I need extra help with** _____

Go to MY SCIENCE COACH *online for help with this subject.*

How Is Distance Measured in Degrees?

When you play checkers, the grid of squares helps you to keep track of where each piece should be. To find a point on Earth's surface, you need a reference system like the grid of squares on a checkerboard. Of course, Earth itself does not have grid lines, but most maps and globes show a grid. Because Earth is a sphere, the grid curves to cover the entire planet. Two of the lines that make up the grid, the equator and prime meridian, are the base lines for measuring distances on Earth's surface. 🔑 **Distances on Earth are measured in degrees from the equator and the prime meridian.**

Measuring in Degrees You probably know that degrees are used to measure the distance around a circle. As you can see in **Figure 3,** a **degree** (°) is $\frac{1}{360}$ of the distance around a circle. Degrees can also be used to measure distances on the surface of a sphere. On Earth's surface, degrees are a measure of an angle formed by lines drawn from the center of Earth to points on the surface. To locate points precisely, degrees are further divided into smaller units called minutes and seconds. There are 60 minutes in a degree and 60 seconds in a minute.

FIGURE 3 ....
Degrees Around
Distances around a circle are measured in degrees.

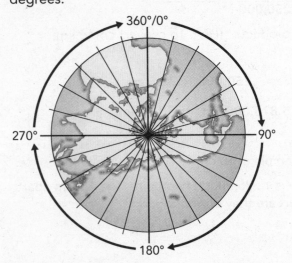

✎ **How many degrees are there in one quarter of the distance around the circle?** _____

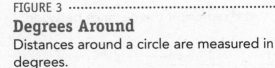

This tangerine is made up of ten equal wedges. The circle shows how the wedges have been grouped into four pieces for serving. Using a protractor, measure the number of degrees in the pieces of the tangerine.

❶ 📐 **Measure** One single wedge has a measure of _____

_____

❷ Two of the pieces are equal in measure. How many degrees does each one measure? _____

❸ The tangerine's biggest piece has a measure of

_____

FIGURE 4 ·······························
Equator and Prime Meridian

The equator and prime meridian divide Earth's surface into hemispheres.

✎ **Measure** What is the angle between the equator and prime meridian?

_____

North Pole

Greenwich, England

Equator

Prime meridian

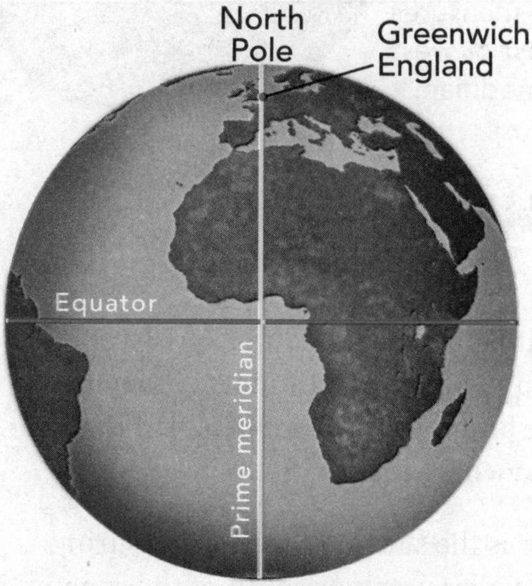

The Equator

Halfway between the North and South poles, the **equator** forms an imaginary line that circles Earth. The equator divides Earth into the Northern and Southern hemispheres. A **hemisphere** (HEM ih sfeer) is one half of the sphere that makes up Earth's surface. If you started at the equator and traveled to one of the poles, you would travel 90°, one quarter of the distance in a full circle.

The Prime Meridian

Another imaginary line, called the **prime meridian,** makes a half circle from the North Pole to the South Pole. The prime meridian passes through Greenwich, England. Places east of the prime meridian are in the Eastern Hemisphere. Places west of the prime meridian are in the Western Hemisphere.

If you started at the prime meridian and traveled west along the equator, you would travel 360° before returning to your starting point. At 180° east or west of the prime meridian, another imaginary half circle lies directly opposite the prime meridian.

Lab zone® Do the Quick Lab
Measuring in Degrees.

🔑 Assess Your Understanding

2a. Identify The _____ and the _____ are two base lines used to locate points on Earth's surface.

b. Explain How are these base lines used?

_____

_____

_____

c. Compare and Contrast How are these base lines similar? How are these base lines different?

_____

_____

_____

_____

_____

_____

_____

_____

_____

_____

_____

got it? ··

○ **I get it!** Now I know that distances on Earth are measured_____

_____

_____

_____

○ **I need extra help with** _____

_____

_____

_Go to_ **my science** **COACH** _online for help with this subject._

15

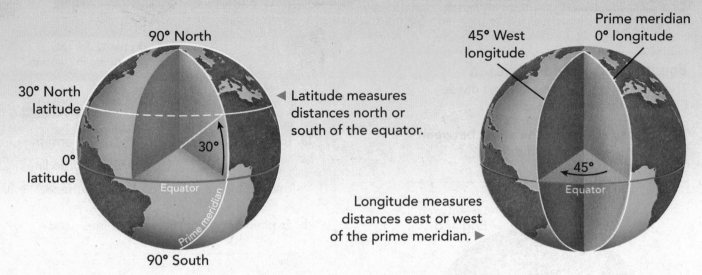

90° North

30° North latitude

0° latitude

90° South

Latitude measures distances north or south of the equator.

30°

Equator

Prime meridian

45° West longitude

Prime meridian 0° longitude

45°

Equator

Longitude measures distances east or west of the prime meridian. ▶

What Are Latitude and Longitude?

Using the equator and prime meridian, mapmakers have constructed a grid made up of lines of latitude and longitude. 🔑 **The lines of latitude and longitude form a grid that can be used to find locations anywhere on Earth.**

Latitude The equator is the starting line for measuring **latitude,** or distance in degrees north or south of the equator. The latitude at the equator is 0°. Between the equator and each pole are 90 evenly spaced, parallel lines called lines of latitude. Each degree of latitude is equal to about 111 kilometers.

apply it!

Every point on Earth's surface has a particular latitude and longitude.

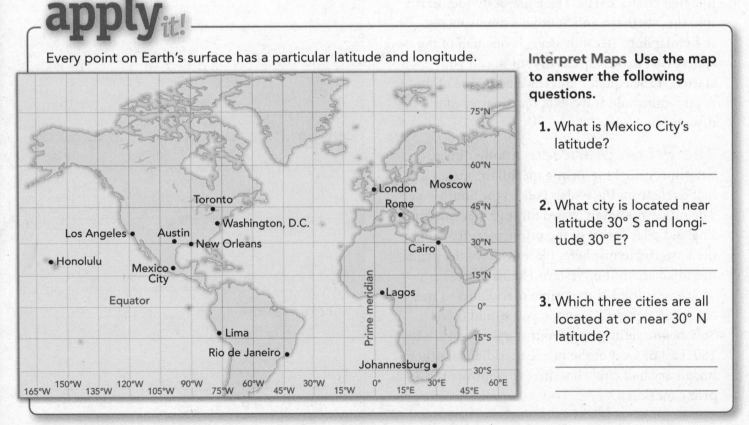

Interpret Maps **Use the map to answer the following questions.**

1. What is Mexico City's latitude?

_____

2. What city is located near latitude 30° S and longitude 30° E?

_____

3. Which three cities are all located at or near 30° N latitude?

_____

_____

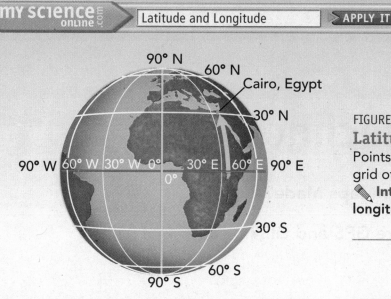

90° N
60° N
Cairo, Egypt
30° N
90° W 60° W 30° W 0°   30° E 60° E 90° E
0°
30° S
60° S
90° S

FIGURE 5 ··

Latitude and Longitude

Points on Earth's surface can be located using the grid of latitude and longitude lines.

✎ **Interpret Maps** What are the latitude and longitude of Cairo, Egypt?

_____

A line of latitude is defined by the angle it makes with the equator and the center of Earth. **Figure 5** shows how lines drawn from the center of Earth to the equator and from the center of Earth to 30° North form an angle of 30°.

Longitude The distance in degrees east or west of the prime meridian is called **longitude.** There are 360 lines of longitude that run from north to south, meeting at the poles. Each line represents one degree of longitude. A degree of longitude equals about 111 kilometers at the equator. But at the poles, where the lines of longitude come together, the distance decreases to zero.

The prime meridian, which is the starting line for measuring longitude, is at 0°. The longitude lines in each hemisphere are numbered from 0° to 180°. Half of the lines of longitude are in the Eastern Hemisphere and half are in the Western Hemisphere.

Each line of longitude is defined by the angle it makes with the prime meridian and Earth's center. As shown in **Figure 5**, lines from the center of Earth to the prime meridian and from the center of Earth to 45° West form an angle of 45° at the equator.

Using Latitude and Longitude The location of any point on Earth's surface can be expressed in terms of the latitude and longitude lines that cross at that point. For example, you can see on the map that New Orleans is located where the line for 30° North latitude crosses the line for 90° West longitude. Notice that each longitude line crosses the latitude lines, including the equator, at a right angle.

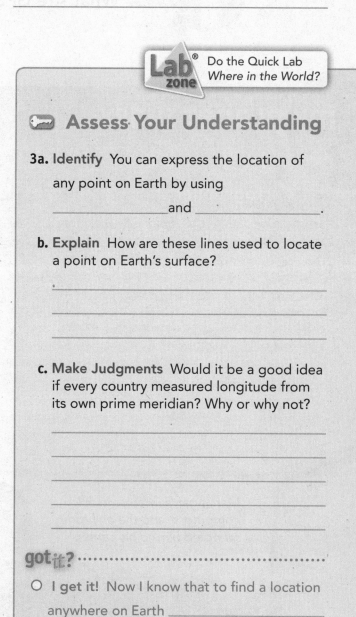

Lab ® Do the Quick Lab
zone *Where in the World?*

🔑 **Assess Your Understanding**

3a. Identify You can express the location of any point on Earth by using

_____ and _____.

b. Explain How are these lines used to locate a point on Earth's surface?

_____

_____

_____

c. Make Judgments Would it be a good idea if every country measured longitude from its own prime meridian? Why or why not?

_____

_____

_____

_____

_____

got it? ·······································

○ **I get it!** Now I know that to find a location anywhere on Earth _____

_____

○ I need extra help with _____

_____

Go to **my science** ⒮ **coach** *online for help with this subject.*

17

UNLOCK THE BIG ?

🔑 **How Are Maps Made?**

🔑 **What Are GPS and GIS?**

my planet Diary

Cartographer

Arie Manangan is a cartographer with the Centers for Disease Control in Atlanta, Georgia. He uses maps to trace the spread of disease and to identify potential epidemics before they begin, helping to save lives. Manangan uses computer software and Geographic Information Systems to analyze the clustering of diseases and to identify factors such as heavy rainfall that might contribute to the spread of disease.

He also makes emergency maps during natural disasters. When, for example, a hurricane happens, public health officials need new maps produced as soon as possible to help in the rescue efforts.

Manangan's interest in art, computers, and the environment led him to his career.

CAREERS

Communicate Write your answer to each question below. Then discuss your answers with a partner.

1. How does Arie Manangan help save lives with maps?

_____

_____

2. Why must new maps be made after a hurricane?

_____

_____

_____

_____

_____

_____

_____

> **PLANET DIARY** Go to **Planet Diary** to learn more about satellite mapping.

Lab zone® Do the Inquiry Warm-Up *Make a Pixel Picture.*

Mapping Earth's Surface

Vocabulary
- surveying • digitizing • pixel
- aerial photograph • satellite image
- Global Positioning System
- Geographic Information System

Skills
🔄 Reading: Relate Text and Visuals
⚠️ Inquiry: Make Models

How Are Maps Made?

For centuries mapmakers drew maps by hand. For example, explorers sketched coastlines as seen from their ships. Then people began to use a process called surveying. In **surveying,** mapmakers determine distances and elevations using instruments and the principles of geometry. In the 1900s, people learned to make maps using images taken from airplanes. By the 1980s, computers had greatly changed mapmaking. Maps that once took hundreds of hours to draw could be produced quickly. 🔑 **Today, computers produce maps using data from many sources, including satellites and aerial photographs. Computers allow mapmakers to store, process, and display map data electronically.**

All of the data used in computer mapping must be written in numbers. The process by which mapmakers convert the location of map points to numbers is called **digitizing.** These numbers are stored on a computer as a series of 0's and 1's. The digitized data can easily be displayed on a computer screen, modified, and printed in map form. Each bit of a digitized image is called a **pixel.** Often appearing as a small square or dot, each pixel represents a tiny piece of the image (see **Figure 1**).

FIGURE 1 ···

Pixels
A digitized image is made up of many pixels.

✏️ **Relate Diagrams and Photos** The grid represents the pixels that form an image. Fill in each square with the pixel color (green, red, or blue) that is dominant.

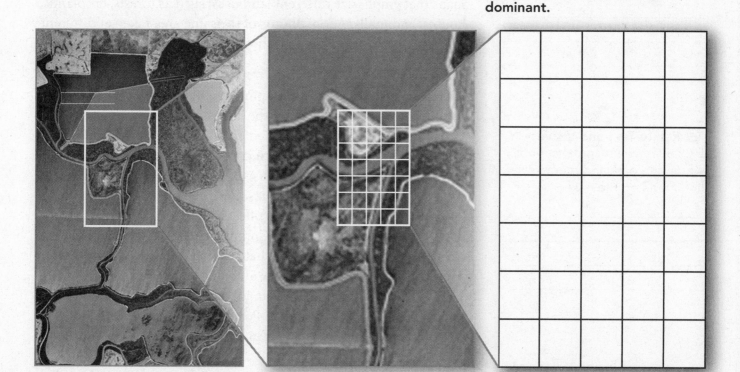

Maps From Aerial Photographs

Much of the data used in mapmaking comes from aerial photographs. **Aerial photographs** are usually taken by cameras mounted in airplanes. As the plane flies, the cameras take pictures of strips of land. Each picture slightly overlaps the next one. Mapmakers then put several pictures of the strips together like a giant puzzle. The result is an image of a wide area. Mapmakers can use this image to make accurate maps. The maps show the correct location of human-made features such as roads and buildings. They also show natural features such as hills, rivers, and lakes.

Aerial photos also provide data on topography, or the shape of the land surface. By combining two photos of the same area taken from slightly different angles, mapmakers can create a three-dimensional image. Mapmakers then trace this image to make a map of the land's elevation and relief.

Aerial photos have many other uses. They can be made into maps that emphasize different land uses, such as forests, croplands, houses, and malls. Aerial photos of the same area taken at different times can be made into a map showing how the area has changed.

Maps From Satellite Images
Computer mapping also makes use of satellite data. Mapping satellites use electronic devices to collect computer data about the land surface. Pictures of the surface based on these data are called **satellite images.** Satellite images are made of pixels, each of which contains information on the color and brightness of a part of Earth's surface. When the satellite image is printed, the computer translates these digitized data into colors.

As a satellite orbits Earth, it collects and stores information about a portion of the surface. Computers use the data to create images. Satellite images show what covers Earth's surface—plants, soil, sand, rock, water, and snow and ice.

Scientists and mapmakers can identify specific features on an image by the colors and shapes. For example, areas covered by vegetation may appear as red or green, water as black or blue, and cities as bluish gray.

FIGURE 2 ·······················

Aerial Photography
An aerial photograph shows information about the shape and features of the land surface. Mapmakers can use the photograph to create a map.

✏️ **Make Models Use the diagram to the right of the aerial photograph to make a street map of the neighborhood. Give names to the streets. Why is it easier to make a map from an aerial photograph than it is to survey the neighborhood on the ground?**

_____

_____

_____

_____

·············· ✏️ ··············

🔄 **Relate Text and Visuals**
Explain how a mapmaker finds water and parkland on the satellite image on the next page.

_____

_____

_____

_____

it!

This satellite image of Washington, D.C., was used to create the map. Study the image and map. Then answer the questions.

1 Identify the numbers on the image that represent these features.

Open space_____

Water_____

Buildings_____

2 Interpret Maps Compare the map with the image. Which one is easier for a tourist to use? Why?

_____
_____
_____
_____
_____

Lab zone® Do the Quick Lab *Reading Satellite Images.*

🔑 Assess Your Understanding

1a. Explain Satellite images use _____ to store data for maps. Each bit of the image is called a _____ .

b. Make Generalizations What are some advantages of computer mapping?

_____
_____
_____
_____
_____
_____

got it?

○ **I get it!** Now I know that maps are made by using _____
_____
_____

○ **I need extra help with** _____
_____

Go to **MY SCIENCE COACH** *online for help with this subject.*

What Are GPS and GIS?

Advancing computer technology has brought new tools to mapmakers. GPS (Global Positioning System) uses satellite data to help users locate their positions anywhere on or above Earth. GIS (Geographic Information System) uses GPS and other electronic sources to display and analyze geographic data.

GPS The **Global Positioning System,** or GPS, is a navigational system that uses satellite signals to fix the location of a radio receiver on Earth's surface. The U.S. Department of Defense set up GPS for military purposes. It is now used by everyone from mapmakers to hikers who need to find the nearest campground. GPS is made up of two main parts: orbiting satellites and a GPS receiver. Twenty-four orbiting satellites continuously send their current location and time to Earth. A user's receiver needs information from at least three satellites to determine its location.

FIGURE 3 ···

> ART IN MOTION GPS Satellites

At least three satellites must be above the horizon to pinpoint a location.

✎ **List** **List five activities in which knowing one's exact location is important.**

_____

_____

_____

_____

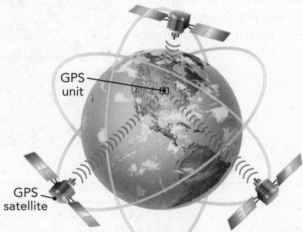

GPS unit

GPS satellite

GIS A **Geographic Information System,** or GIS, is a system of computer hardware and software used to produce interactive maps of many kinds. If you've used online software to get map directions, you've used a GIS. A GIS can use data from many sources, including GPS, satellite images, statistics about an area, and existing maps. For example, a GIS could include data on street addresses, elevation above a river, and rainfall. This GIS could be used to determine the flood risk in a neighborhood.

The different types of information stored in a GIS are called *data layers.* GIS users can combine the information from the data layers to solve problems and answer questions. City planners and scientists often use GIS. For example, they might produce a map made up of the data layers for water wells and old gas stations. Toxic substances from the gas stations could pollute the wells. By studying a GIS map, planners might decide how to protect the wells from pollution.

FIGURE 4 ·······················

REAL-WORLD INQUIRY **GIS Map**

A GIS map often has many data layers to show how the different systems interact.

✎ **Interpret Maps** Shade in the flood plain on the Combined map. On which street would you avoid building houses? Why?

_____

_____

_____

_____

_____

_____

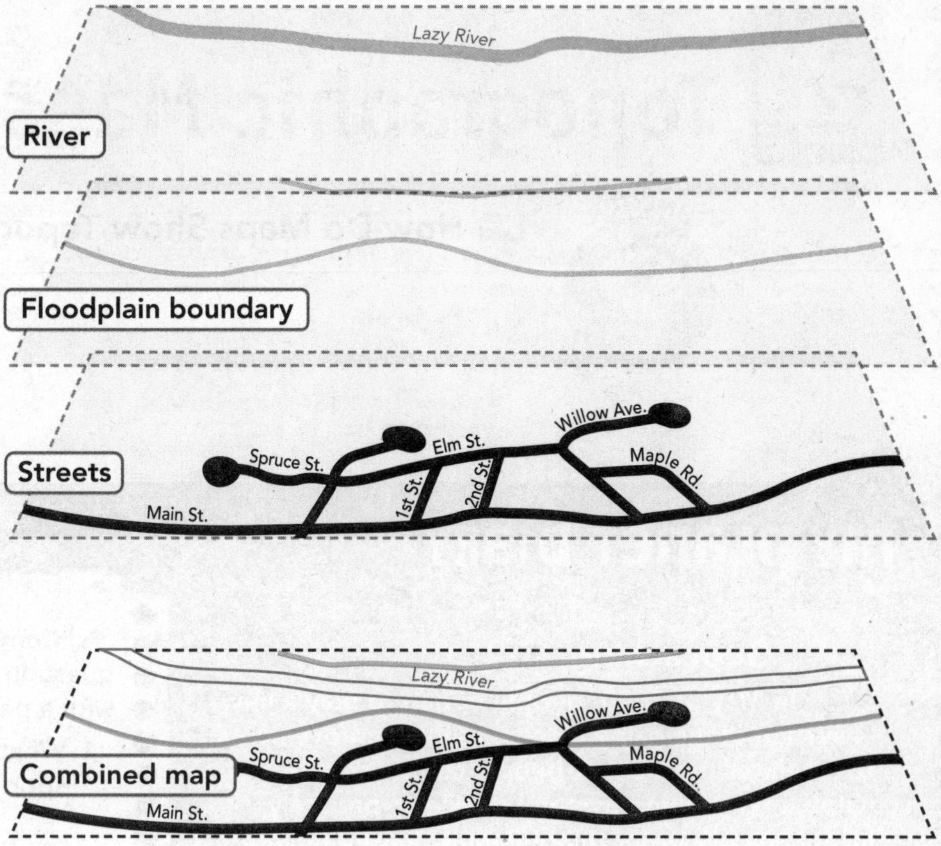

River

Floodplain boundary

Streets

Lazy River

Spruce St. · Elm St. · Willow Ave. · Maple Rd. · 1st St. · 2nd St. · Main St.

Combined map

Lazy River

Spruce St. · Elm St. · Willow Ave. · Maple Rd. · 1st St. · 2nd St. · Main St.

Lab zone ® Do the Quick Lab *Where Are You?*

🔑 Assess Your Understanding

2a. Define GPS has two main parts:

_____ and

_____ .

b. Describe A Geographic Information System, or GIS, can be described as

_____

_____

_____

_____

c. Solve Problems The owner of a chain of coffee shops knows how many people live in an area, the streets where most people drive, and the location of other coffee shops. How can the company use this information and a GIS to figure out where to put a new shop?

_____

_____

_____

_____

_____

got it? ···

○ **I get it!** Now I know that GPS uses _____

_____ and that GIS uses _____

_____

○ **I need extra help with** _____

Go to **MY SCIENCE 💬 COACH** online for help with this subject.

Topographic Maps

 🔑 **How Do Maps Show Topography?**

MY PLANET DIARY

Geocaching

In May of 2000, people began to play a new version of the game hide-and-seek. Improvements to satellites meant that people could use a GPS (Global Positioning System) device to precisely locate any place—or thing. People started hiding objects in the woods or on mountains, and then used GPS data to post these locations on the Internet. They challenged other people to find the objects, and the sport of geocaching (*geo* means "earth"; *cache* means "storage place") was born! With GPS technology, nothing is hidden long, but search-ers still might need to use maps in their quest. A cache can be found anywhere, so people searching for the cache need to rely on topographic maps.

FUN FACTS

✎ **Communicate** Write your answer to each question below. Then discuss your answers with a partner.

1. What technological advance made the sport of geocaching possible?

_____
_____
_____

2. If you were a geocacher, where would you hide a cache? Why?

_____
_____
_____
_____
_____
_____
_____

> PLANET DIARY Go to **Planet Diary** to learn more about topographic maps.

 Do the Inquiry Warm-Up *Can a Map Show Relief?*

Vocabulary
- topographic map
- contour interval
- contour line
- index contour

Skills

↻ Reading: Compare and Contrast

△ Inquiry: Make Models

How Do Maps Show Topography?

A **topographic map** (tahp uh GRAF ik) is a map showing the surface features of an area. Topographic maps portray the land as if you were looking down on it from above. They provide accurate information on the elevation, relief, and slope of the ground.

Reading Contour Lines ⊂⊃ **Mapmakers use contour lines to show elevation, relief, and slope on topographic maps.** On a topographic map, a **contour line** connects points of equal elevation. In the United States, most topographic maps give contour intervals in feet rather than meters.

The change in elevation from one contour line to the next is called the **contour interval.** The contour interval for a given map is always the same. For example, the map in **Figure 1** has a contour interval of 160 feet. If you start at one contour line and count up 10 contour lines, you have reached an elevation 1,600 feet higher. Every fifth contour line is known as an **index contour.** These lines are darker and heavier than the others.

✎

↻ **Compare and Contrast**
Explain the difference between an index contour and a regular contour line.

_____

_____

_____

KEY

Contour interval 160 feet

0 _____ 0.5 miles

0 _____ 0.5 km

6800
7600
Mt. Grinnell
▲ 8,851 ft.
8400
7600
6800
6000
5200

FIGURE 1 ·······
Contour Lines
The contour lines on a topographic map represent elevation and relief.
✎ **Relate Diagrams and Photos** What information does the map provide that the photograph does not?

_____

_____

Mapping a Mountain

FIGURE 2 ·····························

How is a map a model of Earth?

> INTERACTIVE ART

✎ **Interpreting Maps** Study the topographic map and then answer the questions.

1. What is the highest elevation on the map?_____

_____

2. Draw a topographic profile, or side view, of the elevations between Points A and B. Use the index contour lines on the map to plot the points on the graph below, and create your own profile of the mountain.

3. Why would you want to use a topographic map when climbing a mountain?

_____

_____

_____

_____

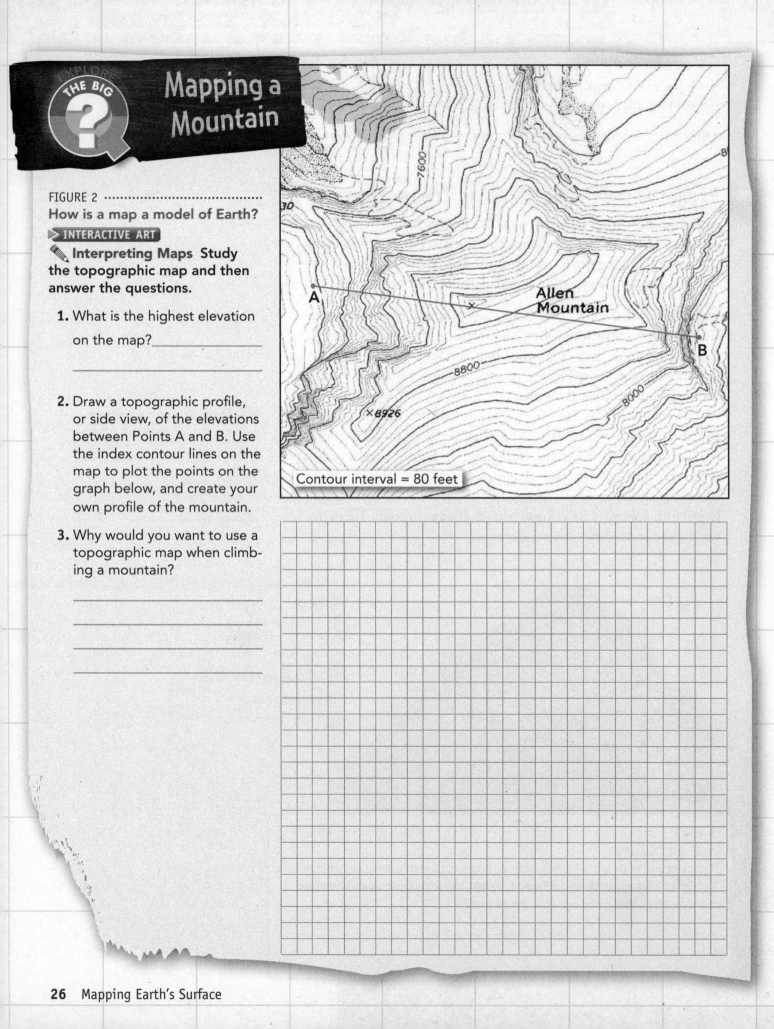

Contour interval = 80 feet

Reading a Topographic Map

Looking at a topographic map with so many squiggles, you may feel as if you are gazing into a bowl of spaghetti. But with practice, you can learn to read a topographic map. First, you must become familiar with the map's scale and interpret the map's contour lines.

In the United States, many topographic maps are drawn at a scale of 1 : 24,000, or 1 centimeter equals 0.24 kilometers. At this scale, maps can show features such as rivers and coastlines. Large buildings, airports, and major highways appear as outlines. Symbols are used to show houses and other small features.

To find the elevation of a feature, begin at the labeled index contour, which is a heavier line than regular contour lines. Then, count the number of contour lines up or down to the feature.

Reading contour lines is the first step toward "seeing" an area's topography. Look at the topographic map on the previous page. The closely spaced contour lines indicate steep slopes. The widely spaced contour lines indicate gentle slopes or relatively flat areas. A contour line that forms a closed loop with no other contour lines inside it indicates a hilltop. A closed loop with dashes inside indicates a depression, or hollow in the ground.

The shape of contour lines also helps to show ridges and valleys. V-shaped contour lines pointing downhill indicate a ridge line. V-shaped contour lines pointing uphill indicate a valley. A stream in the valley flows toward the open end of the V.

Lab zone® Do the Lab Investigation *A Map in a Pan.*

Assess Your Understanding

1a. **Make Models** How does a topographic map serve as a good model of a mountain? What is it missing?

_____

_____

_____

b. **ANSWER THE BIG ?** How is a map a model of Earth?

_____

_____

_____

_____

got it? ....

○ **I get it!** Now I know that a topographic map shows _____

_____

○ I need extra help with _____

Go to **MY SCIENCE** 🔊 **COACH** *online for help with this subject.*

1 Study Guide

A map is a model of Earth because _____

_____

LESSON 1 Exploring Earth's Surface

🔑 The topography of an area includes the area's elevation, relief, and landforms.

🔑 Three major types of landforms are plains, mountains, and plateaus.

Vocabulary
• topography • elevation • relief • landform
• plain • mountain • mountain range • plateau
• landform region

LESSON 2 Models of Earth

🔑 Maps and globes are drawn to scale and use symbols to represent features on Earth's surface.

🔑 Distances on Earth are measured in degrees from the equator and the prime meridian.

🔑 The lines of latitude and longitude form a grid that can be used to find locations anywhere on Earth.

Vocabulary
• globe • map • map projection • symbol • key
• scale • degree • equator • hemisphere
• prime meridian • latitude • longitude

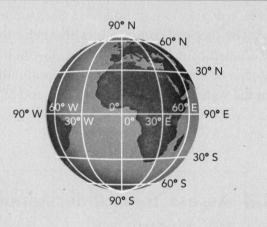

LESSON 3 Mapping Technology

🔑 Computers produce maps using data from satellites and aerial photographs.

🔑 GPS uses satellite data to help users locate their positions on or above Earth. GIS uses GPS and other electronic sources to display and analyze geographic data.

Vocabulary
• surveying • digitizing
• pixel • aerial photograph
• satellite image • GPS • GIS

LESSON 4 Topographic Maps

🔑 Mapmakers use contour lines to show elevation, relief, and slope on topographic maps.

Vocabulary
• topographic map
• contour line
• contour interval
• index contour

Review and Assessment

LESSON 1 Exploring Earth's Surface

1. Which is a landform that has a low elevation and a mostly flat surface?

   a. valley   **b.** coastal plain

   c. mountain   **d.** plateau

2. A landform's height above sea level is its elevation, while its relief is the _____

_____

_____

3. Classify Complete the concept map to show characteristics of different landforms.

Landforms

	Coastal plains	Plateaus
with	with	with
High elevation High relief	____ elevation ____ relief	____ elevation ____ relief

4. Compare and Contrast Compare and contrast a coastal plain with an interior plain.

_____

_____

_____

_____

5. Predict Landform regions feature mainly one type of landform. How would you expect humans to use land in a region of plains?

_____

_____

LESSON 2 Models of Earth

6. The equator divides Earth into two equal halves. What are these halves called?

   a. projections   **b.** degrees

   c. hemispheres   **d.** pixels

7. Infer What is one advantage of a Mercator projection? What is one disadvantge?

_____

_____

_____

_____

8. Interpret Maps What are the latitude and longitude of point A?

_____

_____

9. math! Earth's diameter is about 13,000 kilometers. If a globe has a diameter of 0.5 meters, write the globe's scale as a ratio. What distance on Earth would 1 centimeter on the globe represent? Show your work.

_____

_____

_____

LESSON 3 Mapping Technology

10. The digitized data on a computer map are made up of

   a. scales.   **b.** pixels.

   c. degrees.   **d.** regions.

11. A GIS (Geographic Information System) ana-lyzes geographic data by combining data lay-ers such as _____

_____

12. Make Judgments Why is GPS often more useful than just a map?

_____

_____

_____

_____

LESSON 4 Topographic Maps

13. On a topographic map, how is relief shown?

   a. contour lines   **b.** projections

   c. pixels   **d.** lines of latitude

14. Applying Concepts To show a shallow, 1.5-meter-deep depression in the ground, would you use a 1-meter contour interval or a 5-meter contour interval?

_____

_____

_____

15. **Write About It** Charlene is planning a 5K run to benefit local recycling efforts. She wants the run to be open to all ages and fitness levels. How can she use a topographic map to plan a good route for different groups such as fami-lies with children or regular runners?

How is a map a model of Earth?

16. This map shows part of the Acadia National Park in Maine. The contour interval is 20 feet. Use the map to describe the park's topogra-phy. In your description, identify the elevation of the large lake and Penobscot Mountain, and describe the Bubbles.

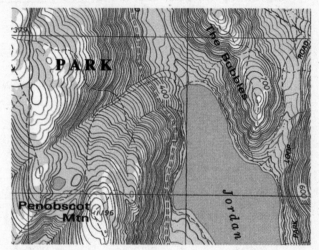

_____

_____

_____

_____

_____

_____

_____

_____

_____

_____

_____

_____

_____

_____

_____

_____

_____

Standardized Test Prep

Multiple Choice

Circle the letter of the best answer.

1. This contour map shows land topography.

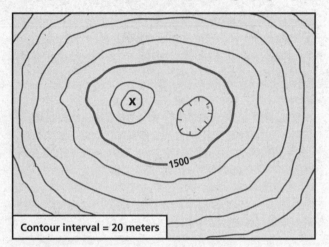

Contour interval = 20 meters

What is the elevation of the point marked X, the top of the mountain, on the map?

A   1,400 meters   B   1,485 meters
C   1,500 meters   D   1,540 meters

2. On a map, what is the term for the height above sea level of a point on Earth's surface?

A   elevation   B   topography
C   relief   D   latitude

3. How is longitude measured?

A   in degrees north or south of the equator

B   in degrees north or south of the prime meridian

C   in degrees east or west of the prime meridian

D   in degrees east or west of the equator

4. Which features could best be viewed on a map with the scale 1 centimeter : 100 kilometers?

A   continents and oceans

B   street signs in a small city

C   hills and valleys

D   neighborhood parks

5. Which of the following describes a plateau?

A   low relief, hilly surface

B   high elevation, high relief

C   low relief, low elevation

D   high elevation, level surface

Constructed Response

Use the picture below and your knowledge of science to help you answer Question 6. Write your answer on a separate sheet of paper.

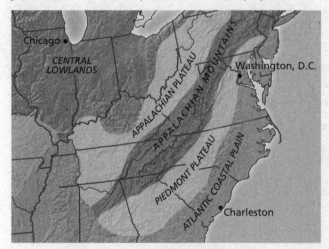

6. Suppose you were to fly from Chicago to Charleston. What landform regions would you cross? How would the land change?

How Much CRUST

Do You Have Over There?

A USGS surveyor takes measurements in Alaska. ▼

If you've ever wondered what exactly was under your feet, you might want to check with the United States Geological Survey (USGS). Since 1897, the USGS has made millions of topographic maps of the United States. The USGS is now the world's largest source of maps of Earth's surface.

The mission of the USGS is to provide reliable scientific information to describe and understand Earth. That's a big job, and it takes more than 10,000 people to do it.

This mission involves more than just topographic maps. USGS geologists also make maps of the thickness of Earth's crust. Take a look at the map below. The crust under mountains, such as the Andes Mountains in South America, is thicker than crust in other parts of the continents. In addition, crust under the oceans, such as the Pacific, is thin compared to the thicker continental crust. USGS geologists have also gathered evidence about the age of Earth's crust. They have learned that thick continental crust tends to be made of rocks that are a billion years old—or more! The thinner ocean floor, by contrast, is much younger—no older than 180 million years.

[Research It] Think about a place you have visited or would like to visit. Research to learn about Earth's crust under this region. What kinds of rocks make up the crust? How old are the rocks? What is the thickness of the crust? Prepare a one-page report about Earth's crust in this region, and illustrate your report with a map or a diagram.

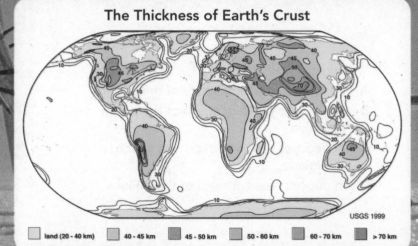

The Thickness of Earth's Crust

USGS 1999

| | land (20 - 40 km) | | 40 - 45 km | | 45 - 50 km | | 50 - 60 km | | 60 - 70 km | | > 70 km |

Setting Sights on Spectacular Sites

You may have seen them near a road, tunnel, or bridge building site, looking through a leveling instrument—a device that looks like a camera on a tripod. Land surveyors collect detailed data about land, such as shape, contour, and elevation, in order to map out what the finished project will look like. They use a variety of mapping instruments from simple measuring tapes to complex satellite photography.

Write About It Research the skills and training that land surveyors need. Write a job posting communicating the skills and training an employer might look for in a land surveyor.

Where Are We?

Centuries ago, people invented navigational instruments for determining compass direction, latitude, and longitude. Mapmakers created the first scientific maps using a magnetic compass nearly 900 years ago. Later inventions, such as accurate clocks called chronometers, helped mapmakers determine longitude accurately. Today, many people use the latest navigational technology, like Global Positioning System (GPS) technology, in their cars! Since the early days of travel and transportation, navigational tools have shaped science and history.

Research It Create a timeline showing a history of navigational devices and how they changed people's ability to travel. Choose one device and write a paragraph explaining how that device works and how it affected navigation and travel.

WHY
DOES THIS
ROCK
LOOK LIKE A
SPONGE?

THE BIG ?

What processes break down rock?

What could make a rock so full of holes? These rock formations, called *tafoni*, are found along the coast of California at Salt Point State Park.

Develop Hypotheses **Explain what you think caused the holes in these rock formations.**

_____

_____

_____

_____

_____

_____

_____

_____

▶ UNTAMED SCIENCE Watch the **Untamed Science** video to learn more about the forces that break down rock.

Weathering and Soil

2 Getting Started

Check Your Understanding

1. Background Read the paragraph below and then answer the question.

The **minerals** that make up a rock determine some of the rock's properties. The properties of a rock can change in two ways: **physical changes** and **chemical changes.** Physical changes change the shape or size of a rock, but not its composition. Chemical changes can change minerals into other substances, changing the composition of the rock.

> **Minerals** are naturally occurring, inorganic solids that have specific crystal structures and specific chemical compositions.
>
> A **physical change** is any change that does not alter the chemical composition of a substance.
>
> A **chemical change** produces one or more new substances.

• How can you tell if a physical change has occurred in a rock?

_____

_____

▶ **MY READING WEB** If you had trouble answering the question above, visit **My Reading Web** and type in **Weathering and Soil.**

Vocabulary Skill

Suffixes A suffix is a letter or group of letters added to the end of a word to change its meaning and often its part of speech. The suffix -ation added to a verb can form a noun that means "process of" or "action of." For example, the suffix -ation added to observe forms the noun observation.

Suffix	Meaning	Part of Speech	Examples
-ation, -sion	Process of, action of	Noun	Abrasion, oxidation, conservation
-ing	Showing continuous action	Noun or adjective	Weathering, plowing

2. Quick Check Circle the correct words to complete the sentence.

• People who (conserve/conservation) energy are contributing to energy (conserve/conservation).

mechanical weathering

soil

decomposer

contour plowing

Chapter Preview

LESSON 1
- uniformitarianism
- erosion
- weathering
- mechanical weathering
- chemical weathering
- abrasion
- frost wedging
- oxidation
- permeable

↺ **Relate Cause and Effect**
△ Control Variables

LESSON 2
- soil
- bedrock
- humus
- fertility
- loam
- pH scale
- soil horizon
- topsoil
- subsoil
- decomposer

↺ **Ask Questions**
△ Form Operational Definitions

LESSON 3
- natural resource
- soil conservation
- crop rotation
- contour plowing
- conservation plowing

↺ **Summarize**
△ Observe

> VOCAB FLASH CARDS   For extra help with vocabulary, visit **Vocab Flash Cards** and type in *Weathering and Soil.*

1 Rocks and Weathering

UNLOCK THE BIG ?

- 🔑 **What Breaks Down Rocks?**
- 🔑 **What Causes Weathering?**
- 🔑 **How Fast Does Weathering Occur?**

MY PLANET DIARY

DISCOVERY

Wearing Away Mars

Does this scene look like a desert? It is—but not on Earth! These rocks are found on Mars. Blowing sand wears away some rocks on the surface. Fog containing acid dissolves and breaks down other rocks. Over time, the rocks break down into small particles, covering the planet with reddish sand.

Lab zone® Do the Inquiry Warm-Up *How Fast Can It Fizz?*

✏️ **Communicate** After you read about the rocks on Mars, answer these questions with a partner.

1. What are two processes that break down rocks on Mars?

_____

_____

2. Give an example of rocks you have seen that were changed by natural processes.

_____

_____

_____

▶ **PLANET DIARY** Go to **Planet Diary** to learn more about rocks and weathering.

What Breaks Down Rocks?

Even the hardest rocks wear down over time—on Earth or on Mars. Natural processes break down rocks and carry the pieces away.

How do scientists know what processes shaped Earth in the past? Geologists make inferences based on the principle of **uniformitarianism** (yoon uh fawrm uh TAYR ee un iz um). This principle states that the geologic processes that operate today also operated in the past. Scientists can infer that ancient landforms and features formed through the same processes they observe today.

Vocabulary

- uniformitarianism
- erosion
- weathering
- mechanical weathering
- chemical weathering
- abrasion
- frost wedging
- oxidation
- permeable

Skills

- Reading: Relate Cause and Effect
- Inquiry: Control Variables

Erosion

Erosion (ee ROH zhun) is the process of wearing down and carrying away rocks. Erosion includes the breaking of rocks into smaller pieces. It also involves the removal of rock particles by wind, water, ice, or gravity.

Weathering

Weathering is the process that breaks down rock and other substances. Heat, cold, water, ice, and gases all contribute to weathering. The forces that wear down mountains like those in **Figure 1** also cause bicycles to rust, paint to peel, and sidewalks to crack. **Erosion works continuously to weather and carry away rocks at Earth's surface.**

FIGURE 1 ....

Effects of Weathering
The Sierra Nevada (below) are much younger than the Appalachians (right). ✎ **Predict How might the Sierras change in the future? Explain your answer.**

_____

_____

_____

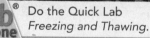

Lab zone Do the Quick Lab *Freezing and Thawing.*

Assess Your Understanding

got it? ....

○ **I get it!** Now I know that erosion and weathering_____

_____

○ **I need extra help with** _____

Go to my science ⑤ coach *online for help with this subject.*

What Causes Weathering?

If you hit a rock with a hammer, the rock may break into pieces. Some forces of weathering break rock into pieces, as a hammer does. The type of weathering in which rock is physically broken into smaller pieces is called **mechanical weathering**. A second type of weathering, called chemical weathering, also breaks down rock. **Chemical weathering** is the process that breaks down rock through chemical changes.

Mechanical Weathering If you have seen rocks that are cracked or split in layers, then you have seen rocks that have undergone mechanical weathering. Mechanical weathering usually works slowly. But over very long periods of time, it does more than wear down rocks. Mechanical weathering, as part of erosion, eventually wears away whole mountains.

FIGURE 2 ····························

> INTERACTIVE ART **Forces of Mechanical Weathering**

✎ Classify **Match each description to an example shown in the photos on the next page.**

CHALLENGE How might more than one agent of mechanical weathering operate in the same place?

_____

_____

_____

_____

1 **Animal Actions**

Animals that burrow in the ground—including moles, gophers, prairie dogs, and some insects—loosen and break apart rocks in the soil.

2 **Freezing and Thawing**

When water freezes in a crack in a rock, it expands and makes the crack bigger. The process of frost wedging also widens cracks in sidewalks and causes potholes in streets.

3 **Plant Growth**

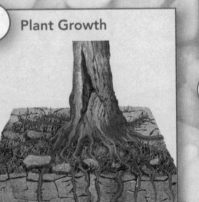

Plant roots enter cracks in rocks. As roots grow, they force the cracks apart. Over time, the roots of even small plants can pry apart cracked rocks.

4 **Release of Pressure**

As erosion removes material from the surface of a mass of rock, pressure on the rock is reduced. This release of pressure causes the outside of the rock to crack and flake off like the layers of an onion.

5 **Abrasion**

Sand and other rock particles that are carried by wind, water, or ice can wear away exposed rock surfaces like sandpaper on wood.

Agents of Mechanical Weathering 🔑 The
**natural agents of mechanical weathering include freezing and
thawing, release of pressure, plant growth, actions of animals, and
abrasion.** Abrasion (uh BRAY zhun) refers to the wearing away of
rock by rock particles carried by water, ice, wind, or gravity. Human
activities, such as mining and farming, can also cause weathering.

In cool climates, the most important agent of mechanical
weathering is the freezing and thawing of water. Water seeps into
cracks in rocks and freezes there, expanding as it freezes. The ice
then forces the rock apart. Wedges of ice in rocks widen and deepen
cracks. This process is called **frost wedging.** When the ice melts,
water seeps deeper into the cracks. With repeated freezing and
thawing, the cracks slowly expand until pieces of rock break off.

Chemical Weathering

Chemical weathering can produce new minerals as it breaks down rock. For example, granite is made up of several minerals, including feldspars. As a result of chemical weathering, the feldspar minerals eventually change to clay.

Chemical and mechanical weathering often work together. Chemical weathering creates holes or soft spots in rock, so the rock breaks apart more easily. As rocks break into pieces, more surface area is exposed to chemical weathering, as shown in **Figure 3**.

Agents of Chemical Weathering

The agents of chemical weathering include water, oxygen, carbon dioxide, living organisms, and acid rain.

Water Water weathers some rock by dissolving it. Water also carries other substances that dissolve or break down rock, including oxygen, carbon dioxide, and other chemicals.

FIGURE 3

Weathering and Surface Area

Weathering breaks rock into smaller pieces. While the pieces are usually irregularly shaped, you can model the process with cubes. The diagram shows what would happen if a rock cube broke into smaller cubes.

✏ **Calculate** By how much does the surface area increase? How would the rate of weathering change?

_____

_____

_____

FIGURE 4 ···············

> ART IN MOTION **Chemical Weathering**

Acid rain chemically weathered the statue of the lion.

✎ **Infer** Which agent of chemical weathering most likely formed this limestone cavern?

_____

_____

_____

Lab zone ® Do the Quick Lab *Rusting Away.*

Oxygen The oxygen gas in air is an important cause of chemical weathering. Iron combines with oxygen in the presence of water in a process called **oxidation.** The product of iron oxidation is rust. Rust makes rock soft and crumbly and gives it a red or brown color.

Carbon Dioxide Another gas found in air, carbon dioxide, also causes chemical weathering when it dissolves in water. The result is a weak acid called carbonic acid. Carbonic acid easily weathers some kinds of rocks, such as marble and limestone.

Living Organisms As a plant's roots grow, they produce weak acids that slowly dissolve rock around the roots. Lichens—plantlike organisms that grow on rocks—also produce weak acids.

Acid Rain Rainwater is naturally slightly acidic. Burning coal, oil, and gas for energy can pollute the air with sulfur, carbon, and nitrogen compounds. These compounds react with water vapor in clouds, making acids that are stronger than normal rainwater. These acids mix with raindrops and fall as acid rain. Acid rain causes very rapid chemical weathering of rock.

🗝 **Assess Your Understanding**

1a. Define (Mechanical/chemical) weathering physically breaks rock into smaller pieces.

b. Classify Circle the examples of chemical weathering. Underline the examples of mechanical weathering. Freezing and thawing, oxidation, water dissolving chemicals, abrasion, acid rain

c. Predict Many ancient monuments are made of marble. Some are located in highly polluted cities. How might the pollution affect the monuments?

_____

_____

_____

got it? ···

○ **I get it!** Now I know that weathering is caused by_____

_____

○ **I need extra help with** _____

Go to **MY SCIENCE COACH** *online for help with this subject.*

How Fast Does Weathering Occur?

Visitors to New England's historic cemeteries may notice a surprising fact. Slate tombstones carved in the 1700s are less weathered and easier to read than marble gravestones from the 1800s. Why is this so? Some kinds of rocks weather more rapidly than others. **The most important factors that determine the rate at which weathering occurs are the type of rock and the climate.**

Type of Rock The minerals that make up the rock determine how fast it weathers. Rocks that are made of minerals that do not dissolve easily will weather slowly. Rocks weather faster if they are made of minerals that do dissolve easily.

Some rocks weather more easily because they are permeable. **Permeable** (PUR mee uh bul) means that a material is full of tiny, connected air spaces that allow water to seep through it. The spaces increase the surface area of the rock. As water seeps through the spaces in the rock, it carries chemicals that dissolve the rock. The water also removes material broken down by weathering.

do the math!

Which Weathered Faster?

The data table shows how much stone was lost due to weathering for two identical pieces of limestone from different locations.

❶ Graph Use the data to make a double-line graph. Be sure to label the axes and provide a key and a title.

❷ Draw Conclusions (Stone A/Stone B) weathered at a faster rate.

Weathering Rates of Limestone		
Time (years)	Thickness of Stone Lost (mm)	
	Stone A	Stone B
200	1.75	0.80
400	3.50	1.60
600	5.25	2.40
800	7.00	3.20
1,000	8.75	4.00

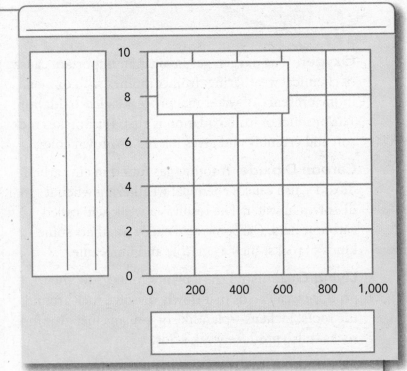

❸ Infer What can you infer caused the difference in the rates of weathering?

_____

_____

_____

Climate Climate refers to the average weather conditions in an area. Both chemical and mechanical weathering occur faster in wet climates. Rainfall provides the water needed for chemical changes as well as for freezing and thawing.

Chemical reactions occur faster at higher temperatures. That is why chemical weathering occurs more quickly where the climate is both hot and wet. Human activities, such as those that produce acid rain, also increase the rate of weathering.

↻ Relate Cause and Effect
Underline the reason that chemical weathering occurs faster in hot climates.

apply it!

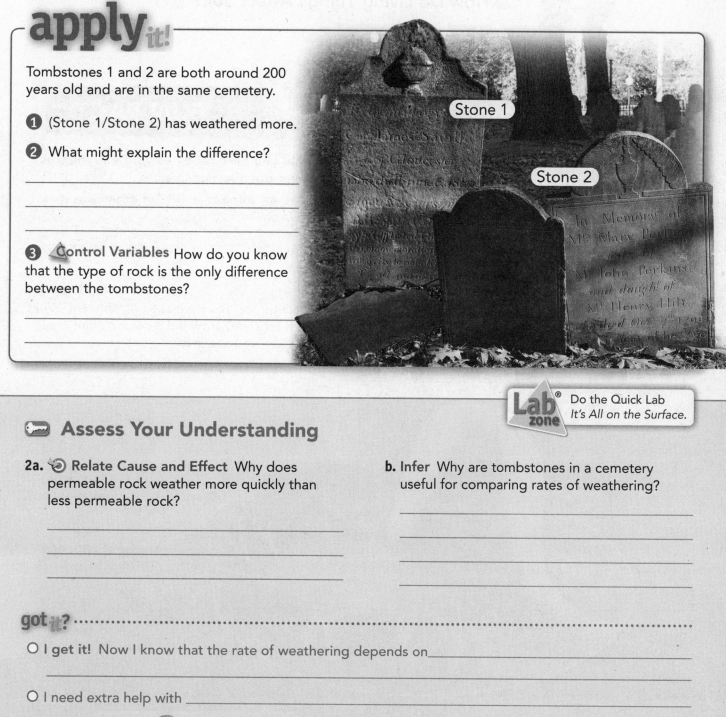

Tombstones 1 and 2 are both around 200 years old and are in the same cemetery.

1 (Stone 1/Stone 2) has weathered more.

2 What might explain the difference?

_____

_____

_____

3 **Control Variables** How do you know that the type of rock is the only difference between the tombstones?

_____

_____

Stone 1

Stone 2

Lab zone® Do the Quick Lab
It's All on the Surface.

🔑 Assess Your Understanding

2a. ↻ **Relate Cause and Effect** Why does permeable rock weather more quickly than less permeable rock?

_____

_____

_____

b. Infer Why are tombstones in a cemetery useful for comparing rates of weathering?

_____

_____

_____

got it? ·······

○ **I get it!** Now I know that the rate of weathering depends on_____

_____

○ I need extra help with _____

Go to **my science** 🅢 **COACH** *online for help with this subject.*

How Soil Forms

UNLOCK THE BIG ?

🔑 What Is Soil?

🔑 How Do Living Things Affect Soil?

my planet Diary

Life Beneath Your Feet

The soil beneath your feet may not look very interesting, but it's packed with life! Many microscopic organisms live in soil and affect the lives of other organisms. Some bacteria, like the *Pseudomonas* shown above, can protect plants from disease. Hundreds of thousands of soil mites can live in a single square meter of soil. And tiny worms called nematodes eat plants, bacteria, fungi, and even other nematodes!

Bacterium

Nematode

Mite

FUN FACT

Use what you have read and your experiences to answer the questions below.

1. What are some examples of organisms that live in soil?

_____

_____

2. Describe soil you have seen or touched. What did it feel like? How did it smell? What creatures did you see in it?

_____

_____

_____

_____

> PLANET DIARY   Go to Planet Diary to learn more about soil.

Lab zone ®   Do the Inquiry Warm-Up *What Is Soil?*

Vocabulary

- soil • bedrock • humus • fertility • loam
- pH scale • soil horizon • topsoil • subsoil
- decomposer

Skills

↻ **Reading:** Ask Questions

△ **Inquiry:** Form Operational Definitions

What Is Soil?

Have you ever seen a plant growing in a crack in a rock? It may look like the plant is growing on solid rock, but it isn't. Plants can only grow when soil begins to form in the cracks. **Soil** is the loose, weathered material on Earth's surface in which plants can grow.

Soil Composition 🔊 **Soil is a mixture of rock particles, minerals, decayed organic material, water, and air.** One of the main ingredients of soil comes from bedrock. **Bedrock** is the solid layer of rock beneath the soil. Once bedrock is exposed to air, water, and living things, it gradually weathers into smaller and smaller particles that are the most common components of soil.

The particles of rock in soil are classified by size as gravel, sand, silt, and clay. **Figure 1** shows the relative sizes of these particles. Together, gravel, sand, silt, and clay make up the portion of soil that comes from weathered rock.

The decayed organic material in soil is called humus. **Humus** (HYOO mus) is a dark-colored substance that forms as plant and animal remains decay. Humus helps create spaces in soil for air and water. Humus also contains nutrients that plants need.

FIGURE 1 ···

Soil Particle Size

The particles shown here have been enlarged.

✎ **Graph** Mark where a 1.5-mm particle would fall on the graph. What type of particle is it? _____

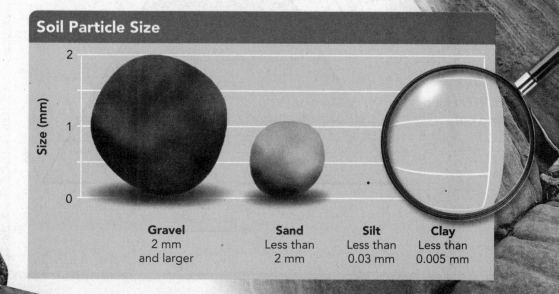

Soil Particle Size

Size (mm)

Gravel	Sand	Silt	Clay
2 mm and larger	Less than 2 mm	Less than 0.03 mm	Less than 0.005 mm

Vocabulary Suffixes How does adding the suffix *-ity* change the form of the word *fertile*?

_____

_____

_____

Ask Questions Before you read the section Soil pH, write a question that you would like answered. Then write the answer.

_____

_____

_____

_____

Soil Fertility

Fertile soil is rich in the nutrients that plants need to grow. The **fertility** of soil is a measure of how well the soil supports plant growth. Soil that is rich in humus generally has high fertility. Sandy soil containing little humus has low fertility.

Soil Texture

Sandy soil feels coarse and grainy, but soil with lots of clay feels smooth and silky. These differences are differences in texture. Soil texture depends on the size of the soil particles.

Soil texture is important for plant growth. Soil that is mostly clay may hold too much water and not enough air. In contrast, sandy soil loses water quickly. Plants may die for lack of air or water. Soil that is made up of about equal parts of clay, sand, and silt is called **loam.** Loam is the best soil for growing most plants.

Soil pH

Soil can be acidic or basic. Acidic substances react with some metals and turn blue litmus paper red. Basic substances feel slippery and turn red litmus paper blue. The **pH scale** measures acidity. A substance with a pH less than 4 is strongly acidic. A substance with a pH of 7 is neither acidic nor basic. (Pure water has a pH of 7.) A substance with a pH greater than 10 is strongly basic. Most garden plants grow best in soil with a pH between 6 and 7.5. Some soils can have a pH as low as 4, which is quite acidic.

apply it!

This diagram is called the soil texture triangle. To use the triangle, first find the percentages of silt, sand, and clay in a soil sample. Then locate each percentage on its side of the triangle. The point where the lines meet tells you the type of soil. (This example shows clay loam soil that is 40% silt, 30% clay, and 30% sand.)

1 Interpret Diagrams What percentage of silty clay loam is silt? (*Hint:* Look at the corners of the silty clay loam area.)

_____

2 Interpret Diagrams A soil sample has 20% silt, 10% clay, and 70% sand. What kind of soil is it? (*Hint:* Draw lines to find out.)

_____

3 Form Operational Definitions How would you define silty clay soil?

_____

_____

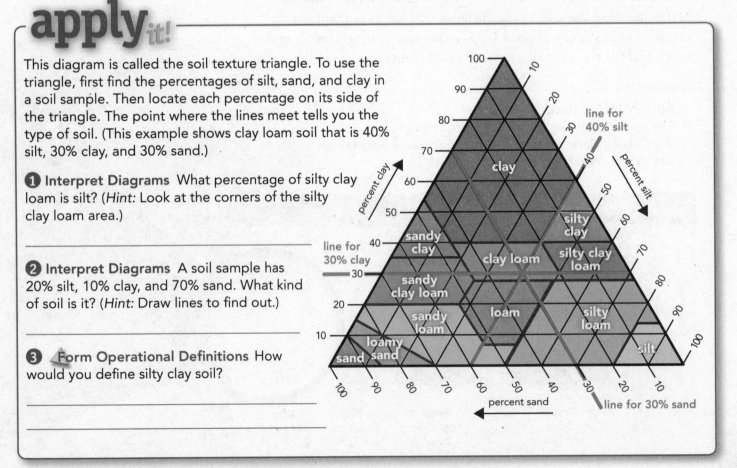

The Process of Soil Formation

Soil forms as rock is broken down by weathering and mixes with other materials on the surface. Soil forms constantly wherever bedrock weathers. Soil formation continues over a long period of time.

Gradually, soil develops layers called horizons. A **soil horizon** is a layer of soil that differs in color, texture, and composition from the layers above or below it. **Figure 2** shows how scientists classify soil into three horizons.

C Horizon The C horizon forms as bedrock begins to weather. The rock breaks up into small particles.

A Horizon The A horizon is made up of **topsoil,** a crumbly, dark brown soil that is a mixture of humus, clay, and other minerals. Topsoil forms as plants add organic material to the soil, and plant roots weather pieces of rock.

B Horizon The B horizon, often called **subsoil,** usually consists of clay and other particles of rock, but little humus. It forms as rainwater washes these materials down from the A horizon.

FIGURE 2 ·······························

Soil Layers

✎ **Use the diagram to answer the questions.**

1. **Compare and Contrast** Which layer contains the most organic material?

   _____

2. CHALLENGE In what climates would you expect soil to form fastest? Why?

   _____

   _____

   _____

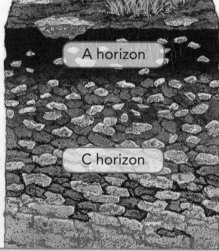
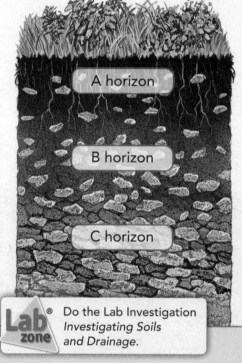

Lab zone ® Do the Lab Investigation *Investigating Soils and Drainage.*

Assess Your Understanding

1a. List What are three characteristics used to describe soil?

_____

b. Compare and Contrast How are the A, B, and C horizons different?

_____

_____

_____

_____

got it? ·································

○ I get it! Now I know that soil forms from _____

_____

_____

_____

○ I need extra help with _____

Go to MY SCIENCE ⑤ COACH online for help with this subject.

How Do Living Things Affect Soil?

Many organisms live in soil. 🔑 **Some soil organisms make humus, the material that makes soil fertile. Other soil organisms mix the soil and make spaces in it for air and water.**

Forming Humus Dead leaves, roots, and other plant materials contribute most of the organic remains that form humus. Humus forms in a process called decomposition. **Decomposers** are the organisms that break the remains of dead organisms into smaller pieces and digest them with chemicals. This material then mixes with the soil as humus. Soil decomposers include fungi (such as mushrooms), bacteria, worms, and other organisms.

Mixing the Soil Earthworms and burrowing mammals mix humus with air and other materials in soil. As earthworms eat their way through the soil, they carry humus down to the subsoil and subsoil up to the surface. Mammals such as mice, moles, and prairie dogs break up hard, compacted soil and mix humus with it. Animal wastes contribute nutrients to the soil as well.

FIGURE 3 ·······························

Life in Soil

✏️ Interpret Diagrams **Label the three soil horizons. Then label each organism** *decomposer, burrower,* **or** *humus source.* **Some organisms may get more than one label.**

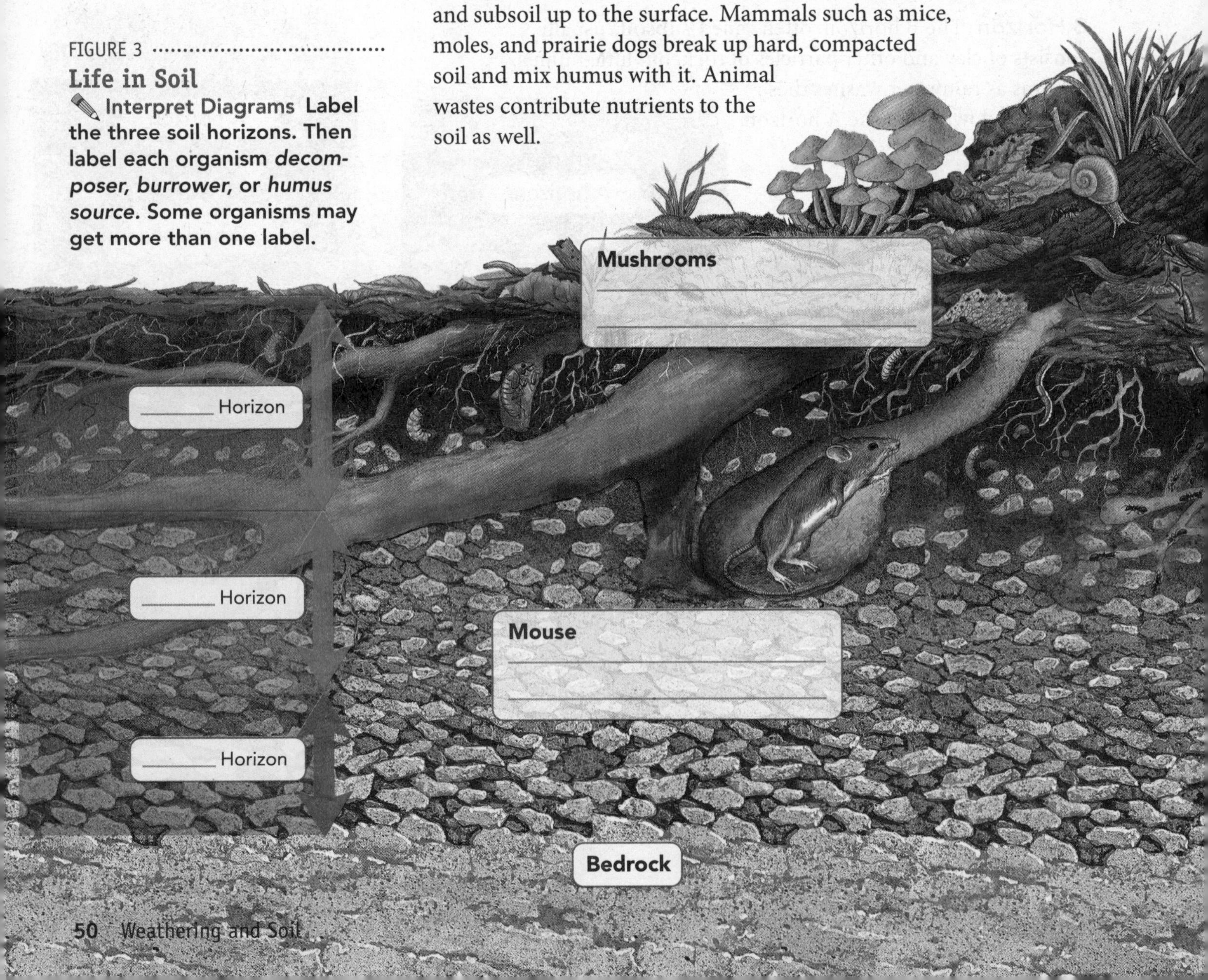

_____ Horizon

_____ Horizon

_____ Horizon

Mushrooms
_____
_____

Mouse
_____
_____

Bedrock

EXPLORE THE BIG ?

From Rock to Soil

What processes break down rock?

FIGURE 4 ···

> INTERACTIVE ART The illustrations show a rock and rich, fertile soil. In the remaining boxes, draw the steps that could change the rock into the soil. Label the processes in each drawing. Include at least two types of weathering.

Dead leaves

Earthworm

Bacteria

Lab zone® Do the Quick Lab
The Contents of Soil.

Assess Your Understanding

2a. Identify Organisms contribute to soil formation by _____ and _____

b. Describe List two types of decomposers.

_____

c. ANSWER THE BIG ? What processes break down rock? Include the processes of soil formation in your answer.

_____
_____
_____
_____

got it? ··

○ **I get it!** Now I know that living things affect soil by _____
_____

○ **I need extra help with** _____

Go to MY SCIENCE ⓢ COACH online for help with this subject.

Soil Conservation

🔑 How Can Soil Lose Its Value?

🔑 How Can Soil Be Conserved?

my planet Diary

The Dust Bowl

In the 1800s, farmers began to settle the Great Plains of the central United States. Some were used to thin, rocky soil. They were excited to find prairies full of thick, rich soil covered with grasses. Farmers quickly plowed up most of the available land. By 1930, almost all of the Great Plains had been turned into farms or ranches.

But as they plowed, farmers dug up plants that held the soil together. Then a long drought in the 1930s caused the soil to dry out. The soil in parts of the Great Plains, including Texas, Oklahoma, Kansas, and Colorado, turned to dust. Without plants to hold the soil in place, it blew away. Wind caused huge dust storms and clouds of black dirt. Farms throughout the central United States were destroyed. The area most affected by this became known as the Dust Bowl.

DISASTER

Look at the photograph and review the information about the Dust Bowl. Then answer the questions below.

1. What happened during the Dust Bowl?

_____

_____

_____

2. Why do you think the Dust Bowl is considered a disaster?

_____

_____

_____

_____

▶ PLANET DIARY Go to **Planet Diary** to learn more about how soil can be damaged.

Lab zone® Do the Inquiry Warm-Up *How Can You Keep Soil From Washing Away?*

Vocabulary
- natural resource • soil conservation
- crop rotation • contour plowing
- conservation plowing

Skills
- Reading: Summarize
- Inquiry: Observe

How Can Soil Lose Its Value?

Today, much of the area affected by the Dust Bowl is once again covered with farms. But the Dust Bowl was a reminder of how important soil is for humans.

The Value of Soil A **natural resource** is anything in the environment that humans use. Soil is one of Earth's most valuable natural resources because everything that lives on land, including humans, depends directly or indirectly on soil. Plants depend directly on the soil to live and grow. Humans and animals depend on plants—or on other animals that depend on plants—for food.

Fertile soil is valuable because there is a limited supply of it. Less than one eighth of the land on Earth has soils that are well suited for farming. Soil is also in limited supply because it takes a long time to form. It can take hundreds of years for just a few centimeters of soil to form.

FIGURE 1 ....
Prairie Grasses
Prairie soils like those found on the Great Plains are still among the most fertile in the world.

✎ **Make Generalizations** Based on the illustration below, how do you think prairie grasses protect soil?

_____

_____

🔄 **Summarize** Write two sentences to summarize the value of soil.

_____

_____

_____

_____

_____

_____

_____

_____

apply it!

The two photos show samples of different soils.

1 ⚠ **Observe** List two visible differences between the two soil samples.

_____

_____

_____

_____

2 CHALLENGE Which sample would you predict is more fertile? (Sample A/Sample B)

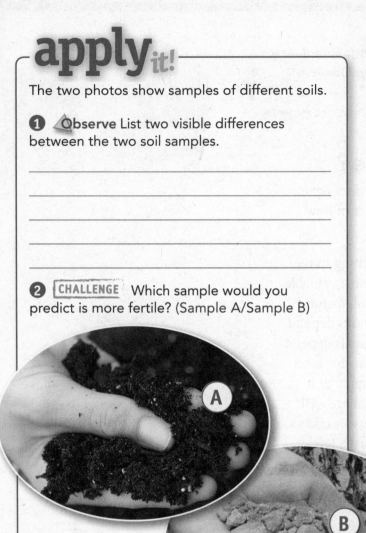

Soil Damage and Loss
Human actions and changes in the environment can affect soil. 🔑 **The value of soil is reduced when soil loses its fertility or when topsoil is lost due to erosion.**

Loss of Fertility Soil can be damaged when it loses its fertility. This can happen through loss of moisture and nutrients. This type of soil damage occurred in large parts of the southern United States in the late 1800s, where cotton was the only crop. Cotton used up many nutrients in the soil, and those nutrients were not replaced.

Loss of Topsoil Whenever soil is exposed, water and wind can quickly erode it. Plant cover can protect soil from erosion in several ways. Plants break the force of falling rain, and plant roots hold the soil together.

Wind erosion is most likely to occur in areas where farming methods are not suited to dry conditions. For example, wind erosion contributed to the Dust Bowl on the Great Plains. Farmers plowed up the prairie grasses that held the soil together. Without roots to hold it, the soil blew away more easily.

Do the Quick Lab
Using It Up.

🔑 Assess Your Understanding

1a. Explain Why is soil valuable?

_____

_____

_____

b. Relate Cause and Effect How does wind erosion affect the value of soil?

_____

_____

got it?..

○ **I get it!** Now I know that soil can lose value when _____

_____

○ **I need extra help with** _____

Go to MY SCIENCE 🔵 COACH *online for help with this subject.*

How Can Soil Be Conserved?

Today, many farmers use methods of soil conservation. **Soil conservation** is the management of soil to limit its destruction. 🔑 **Soil can be conserved through practices such as contour plowing, conservation plowing, and crop rotation.**

Changes in Crops Some crops, such as corn and cotton, take up large amounts of nutrients from the soil. Others, such as peanuts, alfalfa, and beans, help restore soil fertility. These plants, called legumes, have small lumps on their roots that contain nitrogen-fixing bacteria. These bacteria make the important nutrient nitrogen available in a form that plants can use.

In **crop rotation,** a farmer plants different crops in a field each year. One year, the farmer plants a crop such as corn or cotton. The next year, the farmer plants crops that use fewer soil nutrients, such as oats, barley, or rye. The year after that the farmer sows legumes to restore the nutrient supply.

Changes in Plowing In **contour plowing,** farmers plow their fields along the curves of a slope instead of in straight rows. This method helps slow the runoff of excess rainfall and prevents it from washing the soil away. In **conservation plowing,** dead weeds and stalks of the previous year's crop are plowed into the ground to help return soil nutrients, retain moisture, and hold soil in place.

Nodules containing bacteria

FIGURE 2 ···

> REAL-WORLD INQUIRY

Farming Methods

Peanuts (above) are useful for crop rotation. The bacteria on their roots make nitrogen available. Contour plowing (left) is one way to conserve soil.

✏️ **Make Judgments** Which method would you recommend to a farmer who wanted to maintain soil fertility?

_____

_____

_____

Lab zone Do the Quick Lab *Soil Conservation.*

🔑 Assess Your Understanding

got it? ···

○ I get it! Now I know that soil can be conserved by_____

_____

○ I need extra help with _____

　Go to **my science 💬 coach** online for help with this subject.

Study Guide

REVIEW THE BIG ?

Processes of _____ and _____ break down rocks and carry them away.
The broken rocks combine with _____ to make soil.

LESSON 1 Rocks and Weathering

🔑 Erosion works continuously to weather and carry away rocks at Earth's surface.

🔑 The natural agents of mechanical weathering include freezing and thawing, release of pressure, plant growth, actions of animals, and abrasion. The agents of chemical weathering include water, oxygen, carbon dioxide, living organisms, and acid rain.

🔑 The most important factors that determine the rate at which weathering occurs are the type of rock and the climate.

Vocabulary
• uniformitarianism • erosion • weathering • mechanical weathering
• chemical weathering • abrasion • frost wedging • oxidation • permeable

---

LESSON 2 How Soil Forms

🔑 Soil is a mixture of rock particles, minerals, decayed organic material, water, and air. Soil forms as rock is broken down by weathering and mixes with other materials on the surface.

🔑 Some soil organisms make humus, the material that makes soil fertile. Other soil organisms mix the soil and make spaces in it for air and water.

Vocabulary
• soil • bedrock • humus • fertility • loam • pH scale
• soil horizon • topsoil • subsoil • decomposer

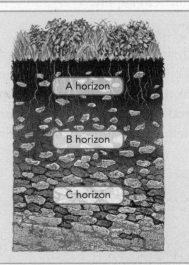

A horizon

B horizon

C horizon

LESSON 3 Soil Conservation

🔑 The value of soil is reduced when soil loses its fertility and when topsoil is lost due to erosion.

🔑 Soil can be conserved through practices such as contour plowing, conservation plowing, and crop rotation.

Vocabulary
• natural resource • soil conservation • crop rotation
• contour plowing • conservation plowing

Review and Assessment

LESSON 1 Rocks and Weathering

1. The process that splits rock through freezing and thawing is called

   a. abrasion.

   b. dissolving.

   c. erosion.

   d. frost wedging.

2. Which of the following is caused by acid rain?

   a. abrasion

   b. dissolving of rock

   c. release of pressure

   d. oxidation

3. Classify Classify each of the following as mechanical or chemical weathering.

Cracks in a sidewalk next to a tree

_____

Limestone with holes like Swiss cheese

_____

A rock that slowly turns reddish brown

_____

4. Predict If mechanical weathering breaks a rock into pieces, how would this affect the rate at which the rock weathers chemically?

_____

_____

_____

5. Write About It A community group wants to build a monument in a city park. They want the monument to last for a long time. They ask you for advice on choosing long-lasting stone for the monument. Write a proposal explaining what factors would affect how long the monument would last.

LESSON 2 How Soil Forms

6. Soil that is made up of roughly equal parts of clay, sand, and silt is called

   a. loam.

   b. sod.

   c. subsoil.

   d. topsoil.

7. The decayed organic material in soil is called

   a. bedrock.

   b. humus.

   c. silt.

   d. subsoil.

8. Identify What are two roles living things play in soil formation?

_____

_____

Use the graph to answer Question 9.

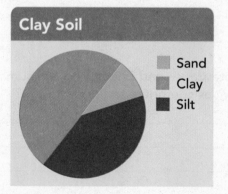

Clay Soil

Sand
Clay
Silt

9. Pose Questions The graph shows a farmer's soil sample. What questions would the farmer need to answer before choosing whether to plant soybeans in this soil?

_____

_____

_____

_____

2 Review and Assessment

Soil Conservation

10. Which technique returns nutrients to soil?

   a. chemical weathering

   b. contour plowing

   c. crop rotation

   d. wind erosion

11. What role do grasses play in conserving the soil of the prairies?

   a. holding the soil in place

   b. increasing wind erosion

   c. decreasing the amount of fertile soil

   d. making nitrogen available to plants

12. Draw Conclusions Why is soil important to people and to other living things?

_____

_____

_____

_____

_____

_____

13. Relate Cause and Effect How did human activities contribute to the Dust Bowl?

_____

_____

_____

_____

_____

14. **Write About It** Write information for a pamphlet explaining to farmers why they should use conservation plowing and contour plowing. Explain how these methods would help conserve soil.

APPLY THE BIG **What processes break down rock?**

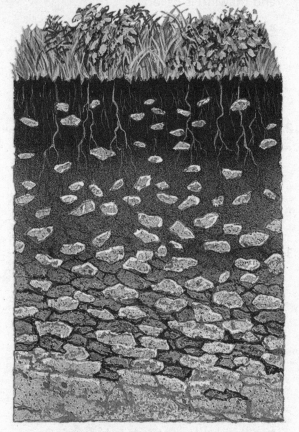

15. Examine the soil sample shown above. Find the A, B, and C horizons. Describe the processes that formed each layer of the soil. Remember to include examples of weathering in your description.

_____

_____

_____

_____

_____

_____

_____

_____

_____

_____

_____

_____

_____

Standardized Test Prep

Multiple Choice

Circle the letter of the correct answer.

1. Use the picture to answer the question.

   What **most likely** caused the weathering shown in the picture?

   A abrasion   B ice wedging

   C plant growth   D animal actions

2. What is the **most** important role that burrowing animals play in the formation of soil?

   A breaking down organic materials
   B decomposing dead animals
   C holding soil in place
   D mixing air and water into the soil

3. Fertile soil is an important natural resource because

   A no new soil can be produced.
   B everything that lives on land depends on soil.
   C there is an unlimited supply of fertile soil.
   D plants cannot grow in fertile soil.

4. In which type of climate would a limestone monument weather **most** quickly?

   A a cold, dry climate
   B a hot, dry climate
   C a cold, wet climate
   D a hot, wet climate

5. A farmer wants to reduce the amount of runoff in his fields. Which of the following methods would be **most** helpful?

   A contour plowing
   B conservation plowing
   C crop rotation
   D topsoil erosion

Constructed Response

Use the diagram and your knowledge of science to answer the question. Write your answer on another piece of paper.

6. Examine the soil samples above. Describe the soil in each pot. Predict whether each soil would be good for growing most kinds of plants and explain your reasoning.

HASTA LA VISTA, REGULAR CONCRETE

▲ The new fly-ash concrete bridge, beside the old metal bridge.

Museum of Science

When engineers had to build a new elevated highway for the San Francisco–Oakland Bay Bridge, they had a lot of things to worry about. After all, if you're going to spend more than 1 billion dollars upgrading a bridge, you want to make sure it will be around for a long time!

The supports of the bridge needed to stand in salt water and mud. Chemicals called sulfates in salt water and soil can weather the concrete and weaken the structure. Sulfates also cause weathering by allowing salt crystals to form on the bridge. But when fly ash is mixed into concrete, it protects the concrete against the weathering effects of the sulfates. Fly ash is powder left behind after coal has been burned. This waste product is usually dumped in landfills.

The engineers of the huge concrete elevated highway used a mixture of concrete and fly ash to build the bridge supports. This improved concrete is helping the bridge to stand up to everything nature throws its way.

Analyze It Identify how weathering has affected a local site, such as a bridge or a monument. Find out what materials were used to build the site, and research what other materials might better withstand weathering. Write a paragraph making the case for using these different materials in future building projects.

THE Plant Doctor

Even as a young boy, George Washington Carver understood plants. Born into slavery in the 1860s, Carver spent his days studying plants. He observed that some plants needed a lot of sunlight and some needed very little. He experimented with mixtures of sand, soil, and clay to find out the kind of soil each plant needed. He knew so much about plants, neighbors called him the "plant doctor."

Carver received a master of science degree from Iowa State Agricultural College and began to teach and do research at Tuskegee Institute. Because Southern farmers grew only cotton, their soil was in poor condition and had started to erode. Carver taught farmers that crop rotation would enrich the soil. Many farmers found that the crops Carver suggested grew better in their soil, and that his methods made the soil healthier. Crop rotation is now a common farming technique.

Research It Dr. Carver taught farmers in the South to plant peanuts, sweet potatoes, and soybeans. The success of these crops often left farmers with more than they could use or sell. Research the many uses discovered by Dr. Carver for one of these crops and present them in a poster.

Dr. Carver inspecting plants in a research greenhouse ▶

WHAT RESHAPED THESE ROCKS?

? What processes shape the surface of the land?

Smooth and colorful, the sandstone walls of Antelope Canyon look more like a sculpture than like natural rock. Located in Arizona, this slot canyon was carved by nature. From above, the opening of the canyon is so narrow that you can jump across. But be careful, some areas of the canyon are more than 30 meters deep!

Infer How could nature have carved these rocks?

_____

_____

_____

_____

_____

▷ **UNTAMED SCIENCE** Watch the **Untamed Science** video to learn more about erosion and deposition.

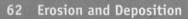

Erosion and Deposition

3 Getting Started

Check Your Understanding

1. **Background** Read the paragraph below and then answer the question.

A giant **mass** of mud blocked the road after a storm. "How did it get there?" asked Gail. "During the storm, the nearby river rose really fast, so the **force** of the water pushed it there," said her dad. "Spring flooding is part of the natural **cycle** of the seasons."

> **Mass** is an amount of matter that has an indefinite size and shape.
>
> **Force** is the push or pull exerted on an object.
>
> A **cycle** is a sequence of events that repeats over and over.

• Why does it take the force of fast-moving water to move a large mass of mud?

_____

_____

> **MY READING WEB** If you had trouble completing the question above, visit **My Reading Web** and type in *Erosion and Deposition*.

Vocabulary Skill

Word Origins Many science words come to English from other languages. By learning the meaning of a few common Latin roots, you can determine the meaning of new science words.

Latin Word	Meaning of Latin Word	Example
sedere	sit, settle	sediment, *n.* pieces of rock or soil moved by the process of erosion
flare	blow	deflation, *n.* the process by which wind removes surface materials

2. **Quick Check** Use the chart to answer the question.
• How does the Latin word *sedere* relate to the word *sediment*?

_____

_____

mass movement

flood plain

glacier

sand dune

Chapter Preview

LESSON 1
- erosion • sediment • deposition
- gravity • mass movement

🔄 **Relate Text and Visuals**
△ **Infer**

LESSON 2
- runoff • rill • gully • stream
- tributary • flood plain • meander
- oxbow lake • delta • alluvial fan
- groundwater • stalactite
- stalagmite • karst topography

🔄 **Identify Supporting Evidence**
△ **Develop Hypotheses**

LESSON 3
- glacier • continental glacier
- ice age • valley glacier
- plucking • till • moraine • kettle

🔄 **Relate Cause and Effect**
△ **Draw Conclusions**

LESSON 4
- headland • beach
- longshore drift • spit

🔄 **Summarize**
△ **Communicate**

LESSON 5
- deflation • sand dune • loess

🔄 **Ask Questions**
△ **Predict**

> **VOCAB FLASH CARDS** For extra help with vocabulary, visit **Vocab Flash Cards** and type in *Erosion and Deposition.*

Mass Movement

○═ **What Processes Wear Down and Build Up Earth's Surface?**

○═ **What Are the Different Types of Mass Movement?**

my planet Diary

DISASTER

Mudflow Hits Town

In December 2007, severe storms hit the northwestern United States. These storms started landslides in the hills above Woodson, Oregon. When landslide debris dammed a creek in the hills, a deep lake formed. If the debris gave way, a mudflow could run downhill and damage the town.

Fortunately, a landowner called the Oregon Department of Forestry (ODF). People were quickly evacuated and a nearby highway was closed. It wasn't long before the pile of debris collapsed, allowing the water to escape. A large mudflow swept away homes, cars, and trees! But thanks to the ODF, no one was harmed.

Do the Inquiry Warm-Up *How Does Gravity Affect Materials on a Slope?*

Discuss the story with a classmate and answer the question.

What caused the mudflow?

_____

_____

_____

▷ PLANET DIARY Go to **Planet Diary** to learn more about mass movement.

What Processes Wear Down and Build Up Earth's Surface?

On a rainy day, you may have seen water carrying soil and gravel down a driveway. That's an example of **erosion**—the process by which natural forces move weathered rock and soil from one place to another. Gravity, moving water, glaciers, waves, and wind are all agents, or causes, of erosion.

Vocabulary

- erosion • sediment • deposition
- gravity • mass movement

Skills

↻ **Reading:** Relate Text and Visuals

△ **Inquiry:** Infer

1 Erosion occurs all the time, even while mountains are forming.

2 _____

4 When new mountains or plateaus form, the cycle of erosion begins all over again.

3 _____

↻ **Relate Text and Visuals**
Read about the cycle of erosion and deposition. Then use what you've learned to narrate the steps in the diagram above.

The process of erosion moves material called **sediment.** Sediment may consist of pieces of rock or soil, or the remains of plants and animals. **Deposition** occurs where the agents of erosion deposit, or lay down, sediment. Deposition changes the shape of the land. You may have watched a playing child who picked up several toys, carried them across a room, and then put them down. This child was acting something like an agent of erosion and deposition.

🔑 **Weathering, erosion, and deposition act together in a cycle that wears down and builds up Earth's surface.** Erosion and deposition are at work everywhere on Earth. As a mountain wears down in one place, new landforms build up in other places. The cycle of erosion and deposition is never-ending.

 Do the Quick Lab *Weathering and Erosion.*

🔑 **Assess Your Understanding**

got it? ....

○ **I get it!** Now I know the three major processes that shape Earth's surface are

_____

_____

○ **I need extra help with** _____

Go to **MY SCIENCE** ⑤ **COACH** online for help with this subject.

What Are the Different Types of Mass Movement?

You're sitting on a bicycle at the top of a hill. With a slight push, you can coast down the hill. **Gravity** is the force that pulls you and your bike downward. It also moves rock and other materials downhill.

Gravity causes **mass movement**, any one of several processes that move sediment downhill. Mass movement can be rapid or slow. Erosion and deposition both take place during a mass movement event. 🔑 **The different types of mass movement include landslides, mudflows, slumps, and creep.**

FIGURE 1 ·······························

▶INTERACTIVE ART **Mass Movement**

✎ **Interpret Diagrams** Read about the types of mass movement. Then match each description with its corresponding diagram.

Mudflows A mudflow is the rapid downhill movement of a mixture of water, rock, and soil. The amount of water in a mudflow can be as high as 60 percent. Mudflows often occur after heavy rains in a normally dry area. In clay soils with a high water content, mudflows may occur even on very gentle slopes. Under certain conditions, clay soils suddenly behave as a liquid and begin to flow.

Landslides A landslide occurs when rock and soil slide quickly down a steep slope. Some landslides contain huge masses of rock. But many landslides contain only a small amount of rock and soil. Some landslides occur where road builders have cut highways through hills or mountains, leaving behind unstable slopes.

A

B

C

D

apply it!

Infer A fence runs across a steep hillside. The fence is tilted downhill and forms a curve rather than a straight line. What do you think happened?

_____

_____

_____

_____

Slumps If you slump your shoulders, the entire upper part of your body drops down. In the type of mass movement known as slumps, a mass of rock and soil suddenly slips down a slope. Unlike a landslide, the material in a slump moves down in one large mass. It looks as if someone pulled the bottom out from under part of the slope. A slump often occurs when water soaks the bottom of soil that is rich in clay.

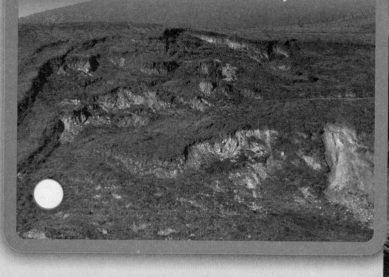

Creep Creep is the very slow downhill movement of rock and soil. It can even occur on gentle slopes. Creep often results from the freezing and thawing of water in cracked layers of rock beneath the soil. Like the movement of an hour hand on a clock, creep is so slow you can barely notice it. But you can see the effects of creep in vertical objects such as telephone poles and tree trunks. Creep may tilt these objects at unusual angles.

Lab zone® Do the Lab Investigation _Sand Hills._

🔑 Assess Your Understanding

1a. Review What is mass movement?

_____

_____

_____

b. Relate Cause and Effect What force causes all types of mass movement? Explain.

_____

_____

_____

got it?

○ **I get it!** Now I know that mass movement is the _____

_____

○ **I need extra help with** _____

Go to **my science** ⓢ **coach** online for help with this subject.

Water Erosion

UNLOCK THE BIG ?

🔑 **How Does Moving Water Cause Erosion?**

🔑 **What Land Features Are Formed by Water Erosion and Deposition?**

my planet diary

FIELD TRIP

The Great Blue Hole

The boat leaves at 5:30 A.M. But you don't mind the early hour because it's the trip of a lifetime: a visit to the Great Blue Hole of Belize.

The Great Blue Hole is actually the remains of a cave formed by erosion. Several factors, including rising sea levels, caused the roof of the cave to collapse. This resulted in a natural depression called a sinkhole.

The Great Blue Hole is more than 300 meters wide and 125 meters deep. It's possibly the deepest and most massive sinkhole in the world. If you want to explore it, you have to scuba dive through the roof. It's an impressive example of what nature can accomplish over time!

Read the story. Then answer the question.

How was the Great Blue Hole formed?

_____

_____

_____

▶ PLANET DIARY Go to **Planet Diary** to learn more about water erosion.

Lab zone Do the Inquiry Warm-Up *How Does Moving Water Wear Away Rocks?*

How Does Moving Water Cause Erosion?

Erosion by water begins with a splash of rain. Some rainfall sinks into the ground. Some evaporates or is taken up by plants. The rest of the water runs off over the land surface. 🔑 **Moving water is the major agent of the erosion that has shaped Earth's land surface.**

Vocabulary

- runoff • rill • gully • stream • tributary
- flood plain • meander • oxbow lake • delta
- alluvial fan • groundwater • stalactite
- stalagmite • karst topography

Skills

Reading: Identify Supporting Evidence

Inquiry: Develop Hypotheses

Runoff As water moves over the land, it carries particles with it. This moving water is called **runoff**. When runoff flows in a thin layer over the land, it may cause a type of erosion called sheet erosion. The amount of runoff in an area depends on five main factors. The first factor is the amount of rain an area gets. A second factor is vegetation. Grasses, shrubs, and trees reduce runoff by absorbing water and holding soil in place. A third factor is the type of soil. Some types of soils absorb more water than others. A fourth factor is the shape of the land. Steeply sloped land has more runoff than flatter land. Finally, a fifth factor is how people use land. For example, a paved parking lot absorbs no water. All the rain that falls on it becomes runoff. Runoff also increases when farmers cut down crops, since this removes vegetation from the land.

Generally, more runoff means more erosion. In contrast, factors that reduce runoff will reduce erosion. Even though deserts have little rainfall they often have high runoff and erosion because they have few plants and thin soil. In wet areas, runoff and erosion may be low because there are more plants to help protect the soil.

Identify Supporting Evidence As you read the paragraph on the left, number each of the factors that affect runoff.

Factor	Example

FIGURE 1 ·······

Factors Affecting Runoff
 Complete the task below.

1. **List** Record the five main factors affecting runoff.

2. **Identify** Using a specific location, such as a park, identify an example for each factor.

3. **Communicate** Explain to a partner what the runoff would be like at your location.

Stream Formation

Stream Formation Because of gravity, runoff and the material it contains flow downhill. As this water moves across the land, it runs together to form rills, gullies, and streams.

Rills and Gullies As runoff travels, it forms tiny grooves in the soil called **rills.** When many rills flow into one another, they grow larger, forming a gully. A **gully** is a large groove, or channel, in the soil that carries runoff after a rainstorm. As water flows through gullies, it moves soil and rocks with it, thus enlarging the gullies through erosion. Gullies only contain water during a rainstorm and for a short time after it rains.

Streams and Rivers Gullies join together to form a larger channel called a stream. A **stream** is a channel along which water is continually flowing down a slope. Unlike gullies, streams rarely dry up. Small streams are also called creeks or brooks. As streams flow together, they form larger and larger bodies of flowing water. A large stream is often called a river.

Tributaries A stream grows into a larger stream or river by receiving water from tributaries. A **tributary** is a stream or river that flows into a larger river. For example, the Missouri and Ohio rivers are tributaries of the Mississippi River. A drainage basin, or watershed, is the area from which a river and its tributaries collect their water.

FIGURE 2 ·
Stream Formation

✎ **Relate Text and Visuals After you read, do the activity.**

1. Shade in the arrows that indicate the direction of sheet erosion.

2. Circle the terms *rills, gully,* and *stream* in the text. Then draw a line from the word to examples of them in the picture.

 Lab zone® Do the Quick Lab
Raindrops Falling.

🔑 Assess Your Understanding

1a. Review How does runoff affect the rate of erosion?

_____

_____

b. Sequence Put these in order of size from smallest to biggest: creek, rill, gully, river.

_____

_____

got it? ·

○ **I get it!** Now I know what runoff does: _____

_____

○ I need extra help with _____

Go to **MY SCIENCE ⓢ COACH** *online for help with this subject.*

What Land Features Are Formed by Water Erosion and Deposition?

Walking in the woods in summer, you can hear the racing water of a river before you see the river itself. When you reach the river's banks, you see water rushing by. Sand and pebbles tumble along the river bottom. As it swirls downstream, the water also carries twigs, leaves, and bits of soil. In sheltered pools, insects skim the water's calm surface. Beneath the surface, a rainbow trout swims in the clear water. As the seasons change, so does the river. In winter, the surface of the river may freeze. But during spring, it may flood. Throughout the year, the river continues to erode Earth's surface.

FIGURE 3 ....

River Erosion

✏️ **Interpret Photos** How does a river's ability to erode change with the seasons? (*Hint:* Look at how the amount of water changes during each season.)

Spring   Summer   Fall   Winter

_____

_____

_____

_____

_____

Water Erosion

Many rivers begin on steep mountain slopes. Near their source, these rivers can be fast-flowing and generally follow a straight, narrow course. The steep slopes along the river erode rapidly, resulting in a deep, V-shaped valley. As a river flows from the mountains to the sea, it forms many features. **Through erosion, a river creates valleys, waterfalls, flood plains, meanders, and oxbow lakes.**

Waterfalls Waterfalls may occur where a river meets an area of rock that is very hard and erodes slowly. The river flows over this rock and then flows over softer rock downstream. Softer rock wears away faster than harder rock. Eventually a waterfall develops where the softer rock was removed. Areas of rough water called rapids also occur where a river tumbles over hard rock.

FIGURE 4

Waterfalls

✎ **Apply Concepts**
Where do you think the layers of hard and soft rock are located? Label the areas on the diagram to show your answer.

Flood Plain Lower down on its course, a river usually flows over more gently sloping land. The river spreads out and erodes the land, forming a wide river valley. The flat, wide area of land along a river is a flood plain. On a wide flood plain, the valley walls may be kilometers away from the river itself. A river often covers its flood plain when it overflows its banks during a flood. When the flood water finally retreats, it deposits sediment as new soil. This makes a river valley fertile.

Meanders A river often develops meanders where it flows through easily eroded rock or sediment. A **meander** is a looplike bend in the course of a river. As the river winds from side to side, it tends to erode the outer bank and deposit sediment on the inner bank of a bend. Over time, a meander becomes more curved.

Because of the sediment a river carries, it can erode a very wide flood plain. Along this part of a river's course, its channel may be deep and wide. The southern stretch of the Mississippi River meanders on a wide, gently sloping flood plain.

Oxbow Lakes Sometimes a meandering river forms a feature called an oxbow lake. As the photo below shows, an **oxbow lake** is a meander that has been cut off from the river. An oxbow lake may form when a river floods. During the flood, high water finds a straighter route downstream. As the flood waters fall, sediments dam up the ends of a meander, forming an oxbow lake.

FIGURE 5 ·········

Oxbow Lakes

A meander may gradually form an oxbow lake.

✎ **Make Models** Draw steps 2 and 4 to show how an oxbow lake forms and describe the last step.

1 A small obstacle creates a slight bend in the river.

Outer edge

Inner edge

2 As water erodes the outer edge, the bend becomes bigger, forming a meander. Deposition occurs along the inner edge.

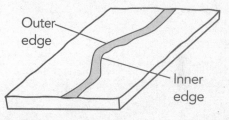

3 Gradually, the meander becomes more curved. The river breaks through and takes a new course.

4

75

Water Deposition As water moves, it carries sediment with it. Any time moving water slows down, it drops, or deposits, some of the sediment. In this way, soil can be added to a river's flood plain. As the water slows down, large stones quit rolling and sliding. Fine particles fall to the river's bed as the river flows even more slowly. 〇━▷ **Deposition creates landforms such as alluvial fans and deltas.**

Deltas A river ends its journey when it flows into a still body of water, such as an ocean or a lake. Because the river water is no longer flowing downhill, the water slows down. At this point, the sediment in the water drops to the bottom. Sediment deposited where a river flows into an ocean or lake builds up a landform called a **delta.** Deltas can be a variety of shapes. Some are arc-shaped, others are triangle-shaped. The delta of the Mississippi River, shown here, is an example of a type of delta called a "bird's foot" delta.

Alluvial Fans Where a stream flows out of a steep, narrow mountain valley, the stream suddenly becomes wider and shallower. The water slows down. Here sediments are deposited in an alluvial fan. An **alluvial fan** is a wide, sloping deposit of sediment formed where a stream leaves a mountain range. As its name suggests, this deposit is shaped like a fan.

Key
░ Mississippi delta

LOUISIANA

MISSISSIPPI

TEXAS

Mississippi River

New Orleans

| 0 | 50 | 100 mi |
| 0 | 50 | 100 km |

Gulf of Mexico

FIGURE 6 ·····················

Deposits by Rivers

✎ **Interpret Photos** Use the pictures above to describe the difference between an alluvial fan and a delta.

_____

_____

_____

_____

_____

_____

_____

Rolling Through the Hills

What processes shape the surface of the land?

FIGURE 7 ···

> **REAL-WORLD INQUIRY** You're a tour guide in the area pictured below, and your tour group wants to learn more about some of the features they are seeing.

✎ **Relate Evidence and Explanation** Identify the two missing features on the image below. Then summarize what you would say about them to your tour group.

Waterfalls and Rapids Waterfalls and rapids are common where the river passes over harder rock.

Tributary The river receives water and sediment from a tributary—a smaller river or stream that flows into it.

V-Shaped Valley Near its source, the river flows through a deep, V-shaped valley. As the river flows, it cuts the valley deeper.

Oxbow Lake An oxbow lake is a meander cut off from the river by deposition of sediment.

Flood Plain A flood plain forms where the river's power of erosion widens its valley rather than deepening it.

Valley Widening As the river approaches sea level, it meanders more and develops a wider valley and broader flood plain.

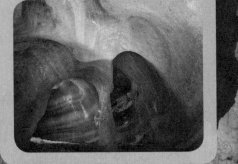
Groundwater Erosion

When rain falls and snow melts, not all of the water evaporates or becomes runoff. Some water soaks into the ground. There it fills the openings in the soil and trickles into cracks and spaces in layers of rock. **Groundwater** is the term geologists use for this underground water. Like running water on the surface, groundwater affects the shape of the land.

Groundwater can cause erosion through a process of chemical weathering. Rainwater is naturally acidic. In the atmosphere, water combines with carbon dioxide to form a weak acid called carbonic acid. Carbonic acid can break down limestone. Groundwater containing carbonic acid flows into any cracks in the limestone. Then some of the limestone dissolves and is carried away in a solution of water. This process gradually hollows out pockets in the rock. Over time, these pockets develop into large holes underground, called caves or caverns.

Cave Formations

The action of carbonic acid on limestone can also result in deposition. Inside limestone caves, deposits called stalactites and stalagmites often form. Water containing carbonic acid and calcium from limestone drips from a cave's roof. Carbon dioxide escapes from the solution, leaving behind a deposit of calcite. A deposit that hangs like an icicle from the roof of a cave is known as a **stalactite** (stuh LAK tyt). Slow dripping builds up a cone-shaped **stalagmite** (stuh LAG myt) from the cave floor.

FIGURE 8 ·····················

Groundwater Erosion and Deposition

✎ **Explain** How do erosion and deposition shape caves? Take notes as you read. Then discuss with a classmate.

Process of Erosion	Process of Deposition

Karst Topography In rainy regions where there is a layer of limestone near the surface, groundwater erosion can significantly change the shape of the land. Streams are rare, because water easily sinks down into the weathered limestone. Deep valleys and caverns are common. If the roof of a cave collapses because of the erosion of the underlying limestone, the result is a depression called a sinkhole. This type of landscape is called **karst topography** after a region in Eastern Europe.

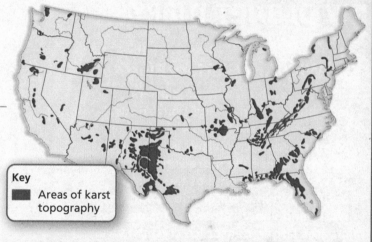

This sinkhole is in Russia's Perm region.

Study the map and answer the questions below.

1 Name three states in which you can find karst topography.

_____

2 **Develop Hypotheses** Why do you think karst topography occurs in these areas?

_____

_____

_____

Key

▮ Areas of karst topography

 Do the Quick Lab *Erosion Cube.*

🔑 **Assess Your Understanding**

2a. List Name two features of water erosion.

_____

b. CHALLENGE What is carbonic acid and how does it affect rock?

_____

_____

_____

c. 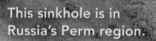 What processes shape the surface of the land?

_____

_____

_____

_____

_____

got it? ....

○ **I get it!** Now I know that features of erosion and deposition include _____

_____

○ **I need extra help with** _____

Go to MY SCIENCE COACH online for help with this subject.

Glacial Erosion

UNLOCK THE BIG ?

🔑 **How Do Glaciers Form and Move?**

🔑 **How Do Glaciers Cause Erosion and Deposition?**

MY PLANET DiARY

Why Are Glaciers Blue?

If snow is white, why do glaciers look blue? When sunlight hits snow, it bounces right back. Snow is made up of microscopic crystals. It is light and not very dense. As more snow falls, its weight turns some of the crystals underneath into water and vapor. The water and vapor refreeze. This process creates larger, denser ice crystals. Over time, the weight of the snow and the ice on the surface makes these crystals even denser. These are the kind of ice crystals that make up glaciers. When sunlight hits glaciers, these dense ice crystals absorb the red and yellow light. Only the blue light escapes!

FUN FACTS

After you read, answer the questions below with a classmate.

1. What makes glaciers look blue?

_____

_____

_____

2. In addition to color, what might be some other differences between snow and glacial ice?

_____

_____

_____

_____

▷ PLANET DIARY Go to **Planet Diary** to learn more about glacial erosion and deposition.

Lab zone® Do the Inquiry Warm-Up *How Do Glaciers Change the Land?*

Vocabulary

- glacier • continental glacier
- ice age • valley glacier • plucking
- till • moraine • kettle

Skills

↻ **Reading: Relate Cause and Effect**

△ **Inquiry: Draw Conclusions**

How Do Glaciers Form and Move?

On a boat trip off the coast of Alaska you sail by evergreen forests and snowcapped mountains. As you round a point of land, you see an amazing sight. A great mass of ice winds like a river between rows of mountains. This river of ice is a glacier. Geologists define a **glacier** as any large mass of ice that moves slowly over land. ☞ **Glaciers can form only in an area where more snow falls than melts.** There are two kinds of glaciers—continental glaciers and valley glaciers.

Continental Glaciers A **continental glacier** is a glacier that covers much of a continent or large island. It can spread out over millions of square kilometers. Today, continental glaciers cover about 10 percent of Earth's land. They cover Antarctica and most of Greenland. ☞ **Continental glaciers can flow in all directions as they move.** They spread out much as pancake batter spreads out in a frying pan. Many times in the past, continental glaciers have covered larger parts of Earth's surface. These times are known as **ice ages.** About 1 million years ago, continental glaciers covered nearly one third of Earth's land. The glaciers advanced and retreated, or melted back, several times. They most recently retreated about 10,000 years ago.

FIGURE 1 ·······················
Continental Glaciers
You're traveling across Antarctica from Point A to Point H on the route below. The cross section shows changes in the ice sheet along your journey.

✎ **Interpret Diagrams** What changes in elevation and ice depth will you encounter?

_____
_____
_____
_____
_____
_____
_____
_____
_____
_____
_____
_____

Depth of Ice (km)

3 — | | F | | G
2 — | B | C | | | East Antarctica ice sheet | G
1 — | West Antarctica ice sheet | D | Ross ice shelf | E
A 0 — | | | | Sea level | H
−1 —

0   500   1,000   1,500   2,000   2,500   3,000   3,500   4,000   4,500   5,000

Distance (km)

Valley Glaciers

A **valley glacier** is a long, narrow glacier that forms when snow and ice build up high in a mountain valley. The sides of mountains keep these glaciers from spreading out in all directions. Instead, they usually move down valleys that have already been cut by rivers. Valley glaciers are found on many high mountains. Although they are much smaller than continental glaciers, valley glaciers can be tens of kilometers long.

High in mountain valleys, temperatures rarely rise above freezing. Snow builds up year after year. The weight of more and more snow compacts the snow at the bottom into ice. **Gravity constantly pulls a glacier downhill.** Once the layer of snow and ice is more than about 30 to 40 meters deep, the glacier begins to move.

Valley glaciers flow at a rate of a few centimeters to a few meters per day. But a valley glacier that surges, or slides quickly, can move as much as 6 kilometers in a year.

apply it!

When glaciers recede, they leave behind evidence of their existence.

❶ **Observe** What was the landscape like before glaciers formed?

_____

_____

❷ **Draw Conclusions** What did the glaciers do to the area?

_____

_____

_____

Before glaciers form   **After glaciers have melted**

Do the Quick Lab
Surging Glaciers.

Assess Your Understanding

got it?

○ **I get it!** Now I know that glaciers differ in how they move: _____

_____

○ **I need extra help with** _____

Go to MY SCIENCE **COACH** *online for help with this subject.*

How Do Glaciers Cause Erosion and Deposition?

The movement of a glacier changes the land beneath it. Although glaciers work slowly, they are a major force of erosion. **The two processes by which glaciers erode the land are plucking and abrasion.**

Glacial Erosion As a glacier flows over the land, it picks up rocks in a process called **plucking**. Beneath a glacier, the weight of the ice can break rocks apart. These rock fragments freeze to the bottom of the glacier. When the glacier moves, it carries the rocks with it, as shown in **Figure 2**. Plucking can move huge boulders.

Many rocks remain on the bottom of the glacier, and the glacier drags them across the land. This process, called abrasion, gouges and scratches the bedrock.

Bedrock

FIGURE 2 ....

Glacial Erosion

✎ **After you read about glaciers, do the activity.**

1. **Identify** Draw an arrow in the diagram above to show the direction the ice is moving.

2. **Explain** In your own words, describe the glacial erosion taking place in the diagram.

_____

_____

_____

_____

_____

83

Relate Cause and Effect As you read, underline the cause of glacial deposition and circle the effects.

Glacial Deposition A glacier gathers a huge amount of rock and soil as it erodes the land in its path. **When a glacier melts, it deposits the sediment it eroded from the land, creating various landforms.** These landforms remain for thousands of years after the glacier has melted. The mixture of sediments that a glacier deposits directly on the surface is called **till.** Till is made up of particles of many different sizes. Clay, silt, sand, gravel, and boulders can all be found in till.

The till deposited at the edges of a glacier forms a ridge called a **moraine.** A terminal moraine is the ridge of till at the farthest point reached by a glacier. Part of Long Island in New York is a terminal moraine from the continental glaciers of the last ice age.

Retreating glaciers also create features called kettles. A **kettle** is a small depression that forms when a chunk of ice is left in glacial till. When the ice melts, the kettle remains. The continental glacier of the last ice age left behind many kettles. Kettles often fill with water, forming small ponds or lakes called kettle lakes. Such lakes are common in areas such as Wisconsin, that were once covered with ice.

FIGURE 3 ·······················

> ART IN MOTION Glacial Landforms

After you read, complete this activity.

1. **Classify** Identify the features of erosion and deposition in the scene below. Record your answers in the boxes provided on the next page.

2. CHALLENGE Identify the feature in the photo on the next page. Describe how it formed.

Cirque A cirque is a bowl-shaped hollow eroded by a glacier.

Horn When glaciers carve away the sides of a mountain, the result is a horn, a sharpened peak.

Fiord A fiord forms when the level of the sea rises, filling a valley once cut by a glacier.

Arête An arête is a sharp ridge separating two cirques.

Glaciers have shaped the land in
Denali National Park, Alaska.

Features of Erosion	Features of Deposition	Photo Feature

Glacial Lake Glaciers may leave behind large lakes in long basins.

U-Shaped Valley A flowing glacier scoops out a U-shaped valley.

Moraine A moraine forms where a glacier deposits a mound or a ridge.

Drumlin A drumlin is a long mound of till that is smoothed in the direction of the glacier's flow.

Kettle Lake A kettle lake forms when a depression left in till by melting ice fills with water.

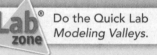

Do the Quick Lab
Modeling Valleys.

🔑 Assess Your Understanding

1a. Review How do glaciers erode by abrasion?

_____

_____

b. Describe How does a moraine form?

_____

_____

got it? ....

○ I get it! Now I know that glaciers shape the landscape through the processes of _____

_____

_____

○ I need extra help with _____

_____

Go to MY SCIENCE 🅢 COACH *online for help with this subject.*

85

Wave Erosion

🔑 **How Do Waves Cause Erosion and Deposition?**

MY PLANET DIARY

Posted by: Lila

Location: Camden, Maine

I was returning home from an island picnic on our 24-foot motor boat, when the wind whipped up. The water in the bay became rough. The waves were splashing up the sides of the boat. Even though my dad slowed down, our boat slammed into wave after wave. My head hit the ceiling of the cabin, as I got bounced each time the boat hit a wave. Anything not strapped down slipped toward the back of the boat. It was scary!

BLOG

After you read about Lila's trip, answer the question.

How did the waves affect Lila's boat ride?

_____

_____

_____

 **PLANET DIARY** Go to **Planet Diary** to learn more about wave erosion and deposition.

Lab zone Do the Inquiry Warm-Up *What Is Sand Made Of?*

How Do Waves Cause Erosion and Deposition?

The energy in waves comes from the wind. When the wind makes contact with the water some of its energy transfers to the water, forming waves. As a wave approaches land the water becomes shallower. The friction between the wave and the bottom causes the wave to slow down, and the water moves forward as the wave breaks. This forward-moving water provides the force that shapes the land along the shoreline.

Vocabulary
- headland
- beach
- longshore drift
- spit

Skills
- Reading: Summarize
- Inquiry: Communicate

Erosion by Waves

Waves shape the coast through erosion by breaking down rock and moving sand and other sediment. One way waves erode the land is by impact. Large waves can hit rocks along the shore with great force. This energy in waves can break apart rocks. Over time, waves can make small cracks larger. Eventually, the waves cause pieces of rock to break off. Waves also erode by abrasion. As a wave approaches shallow water, it picks up sediment, including sand and gravel. This sediment is carried forward by the wave. When the wave hits land, the sediment wears away rock like sandpaper wearing away wood.

Waves coming to shore gradually change direction. The change in direction occurs as different parts of a wave begin to drag on the bottom. The waves in **Figure 1** change direction as they approach the shore. The energy of these waves is concentrated on headlands. A **headland** is a part of the shore that sticks out into the ocean. It is made of harder rock that resists erosion by the waves. But, over time, waves erode the headlands and even out the shoreline.

Summarize Read the text about wave erosion and explain how a wave erodes by abrasion.

_____

_____

_____

_____

_____

FIGURE 1 ·······················

Wave Erosion

✎ **Identify** Shade in the arrows that indicate where the greatest energy of the waves is concentrated.

Headland

Deposition

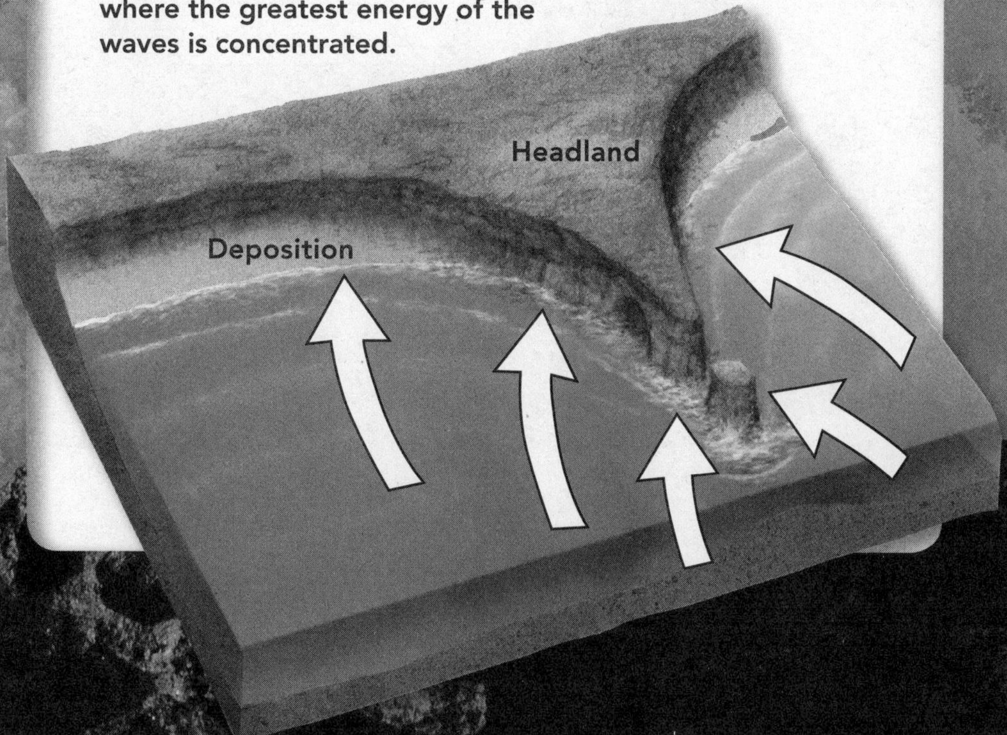

Landforms Created by Wave Erosion Think of an ax striking the trunk of a tree. The cut gets bigger and deeper with each strike of the blade. Finally the tree falls. In a similar way, ocean waves that hit a steep, rocky coast erode the base of the land there. Where the rock is softer, the waves erode the land faster. Over time the waves may erode a hollow area in the rock called a sea cave. Eventually, waves may erode the base of a cliff so much that the rock above collapses. The result is a wave-cut cliff. A sea arch is another feature of wave erosion that forms when waves erode a layer of softer rock that underlies a layer of harder rock. If an arch collapses, a pillar of rock called a sea stack may result.

Deposits by Waves Deposition occurs when waves slow down, causing the water to drop its sediment. **Waves shape a coast when they deposit sediment, forming coastal features such as beaches, sandbars, barrier beaches, and spits.**

1 Beaches A **beach** is an area of wave-washed sediment along a coast. The sediment deposited on beaches is usually sand. Most sand comes from rivers that carry eroded particles of rock to the ocean. Some beaches are made of small fragments of coral or seashells piled up by wave action. Florida has many such beaches.

Waves usually hit the beach at an angle, creating a current that runs parallel to the coastline. As waves repeatedly hit the beach, some of the beach sediment moves down the beach with the current, in a process called **longshore drift**.

FIGURE 2 ···

> INTERACTIVE ART **The Changing Coast**

✎ **Apply Concepts** Use what you've learned about features of wave erosion and deposition to complete the activity.

1. Identify the landforms above. Label them in the spaces on the art.

2. Write an *E* or a *D* in each circle to indicate whether the landform was shaped by erosion or deposition.

2 Sandbars and Barrier Islands Incoming waves carrying sand may build up sandbars, long ridges of sand parallel to the shore. A barrier island is similar to a sandbar. A barrier island forms when storm waves pile up large amounts of sand above sea level, forming a long, narrow island parallel to the coast. Barrier islands are found in many places along the Atlantic coast of the United States, such as the Outer Banks of North Carolina. People have built homes on many of these barrier islands. But the storm waves that build up the islands can also wash them away. Barrier island communities must be prepared for the damage that hurricanes and other storms can bring.

Communicate How could a sea cave become a sea arch? Discuss with a classmate and write your conclusions below.

_____

_____

_____

_____

_____

Sediment

Longshore drift

3 Spits One result of longshore drift is the formation of a **spit.** A spit is a beach that projects like a finger out into the water. Spits form as a result of deposition by longshore drift. Spits occur where a headland or other obstacle interrupts longshore drift, or where the coast turns abruptly.

Lab Do the Quick Lab
zone *Shaping a Coastline.*

🔑 Assess Your Understanding

1a. Identify List two ways waves erode rock.

_____

b. List What are two features formed by wave depostion?

_____

_____

got it? ·······································

○ **I get it!** Now I know that waves shape the

coast by _____

_____

○ **I need extra help with** _____

Go to MY SCIENCE ⑤ COACH *online for help with this subject.*

Wind Erosion

🔑 **How Does Wind Cause Erosion and Deposition?**

MY PLANET DiARY

Saving the Navajo Rangelands

How does wind erosion affect humans? You don't have to go far to find out. In the Southwest, sand dunes cover one third of Navajo Nation lands where sheep and cattle graze. Increasing drought is harming the plants that hold the dunes in place. As a result, the wind is moving the dunes on the Navajo range-lands. This makes it harder for living things to survive. Geologist Margaret Hiza Redsteer studies wind erosion. She left the Navajo Nation land to attend college, but she's come back to help. Recently, Dr. Redsteer met with Chinese scientists to learn how they stabilize dunes. Now, she'll use these methods to help slow erosion on the Navajo rangelands.

Lab zone® Do the Inquiry Warm-Up *How Does Moving Air Affect Sediment?*

CAREERS

Read about Dr. Margaret Hiza Redsteer and answer the questions with a classmate.

1. Why are the dunes eroding on the Navajo land?

_____

_____

_____

2. Do you think it's important for scientists to problem solve together? Explain.

_____

_____

_____

_____

_____

> **PLANET DIARY** Go to **Planet Diary** to learn more about wind erosion.

How Does Wind Cause Erosion and Deposition?

Wind can be a powerful force in shaping the land in areas where there are few plants to hold the soil in place. In the east African nation of Eritrea, sandstorms like the one in the photo are common. Strong winds blowing over loose soil can reduce visibility.

Vocabulary
- deflation
- loess
- sand dune

Skills
- Reading: Ask Questions
- Inquiry: Predict

Deflation Wind causes erosion mainly by deflation. Geologists define **deflation** as the process by which wind removes surface materials. You can see the process of deflation in **Figure 1.** When wind blows over the land, it picks up the smallest particles of sediment, such as clay and silt. The stronger the wind, the larger the particles it can pick up. Slightly heavier particles, such as sand, might skip or bounce for a short distance. But sand soon falls back to the ground. Strong winds can roll heavier sediment particles over the ground. In deserts, deflation can sometimes create an area of rock fragments called *desert pavement.* There, wind has blown away the smaller sediment, leaving behind rocky materials.

Abrasion Abrasion by wind-carried sand can polish rock, but it causes relatively little erosion. Geologists think that most desert landforms are the result of weathering and water erosion.

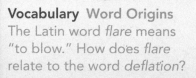

Vocabulary Word Origins
The Latin word *flare* means "to blow." How does *flare* relate to the word *deflation*?

_____

_____

FIGURE 1 ·······························

Wind Erosion
The image shows three ways that wind moves particles.

✎ **Apply Concepts** After you read, complete the activity.

1. In each circle, draw the particles that would be moved by the wind. (*Hint:* Use the key.)

2. Complete each sentence with one of the following words: fine, medium, large.

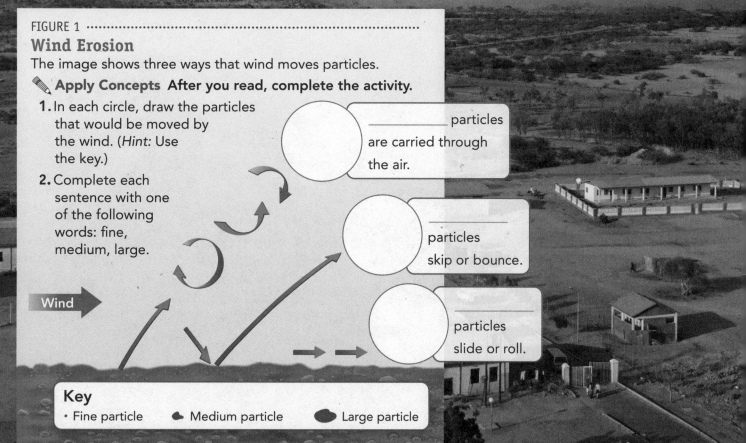

Wind

_____ particles are carried through the air.

_____ particles skip or bounce.

_____ particles slide or roll.

Key
- • Fine particle
- ◆ Medium particle
- ⬤ Large particle

✎

Ask Questions Read the headings on this page, then write down one question you have. After you read, try to answer your question.

_____

_____

_____

_____

FIGURE 2 ....

Dune Formation

✎ **Draw Conclusions** Why do these dunes have different shapes?

_____

_____

_____

_____

_____

Deposits by Wind All the sediment picked up by wind eventually falls to the ground. This happens when the wind slows down or an obstacle, such as a boulder or a clump of grass, traps the windblown sand sediment. 🔑 **Wind erosion and deposition may form sand dunes and loess deposits.** When the wind meets an obstacle, the result is usually a deposit of windblown sand called a **sand dune.** The shape of sand dunes is determined by the direction of the wind, the amount of sand, and the presence of plants.

Sand Dunes You can see sand dunes on beaches and in deserts where wind-blown sediment has built up. Sand dunes come in many shapes and sizes. Some are long, with parallel ridges, while others are U-shaped. They can also be very small or very large. Some sand dunes in China are 500 meters high. Sand dunes move over time. Little by little, the sand shifts with the wind from one side of the dune to the other. Sometimes plants begin growing on a dune. Plant roots can help to anchor the dune in one place.

Loess Deposits Sediment that is smaller than sand, such as particles of clay and silt, is dropped far from its source in large deposits. This fine, wind-deposited sediment is **loess** (LOH es). There are large loess deposits in central China and in states such as Nebraska, South Dakota, Iowa, Missouri, and Illinois. Loess helps to form fertile soil. Many areas with thick loess deposits are valuable farmlands.

Crescent-shaped dunes

Wind direction

Star-shaped dunes

apply it!

Look at the photos and answer the questions with a classmate.

1 **Predict** Which dune do you think is likely to erode faster? Why?

_____

_____

_____

_____

2 Why do you think plants grew on Dune B?

_____

_____

3 How could sand dunes be held in place to prevent them from drifting onto a parking lot?

_____

_____

_____

_____

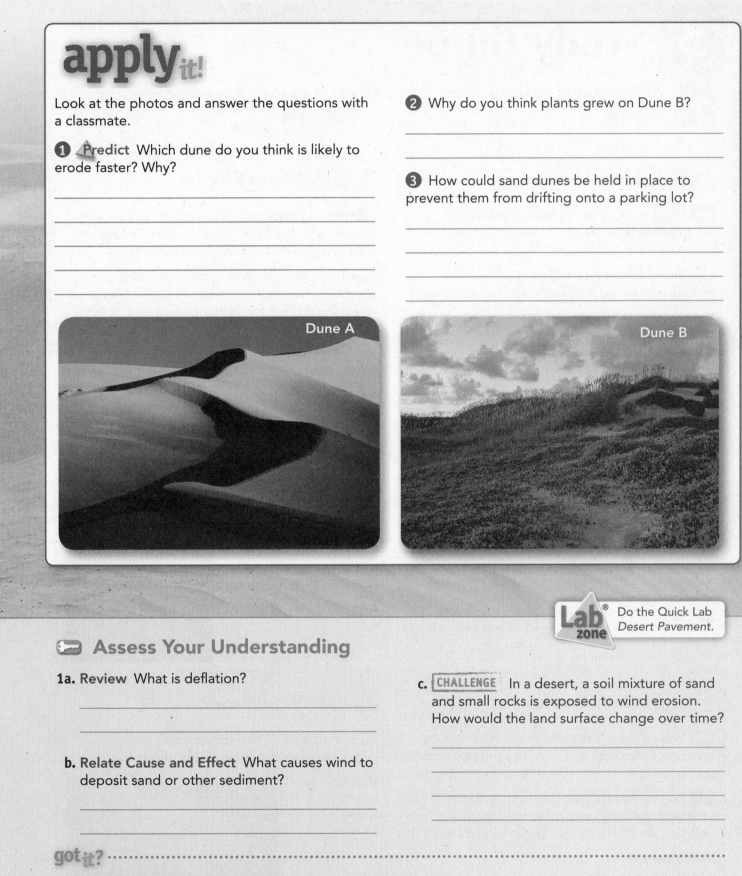

Dune A

Dune B

Lab zone Do the Quick Lab *Desert Pavement.*

🔑 Assess Your Understanding

1a. Review What is deflation?

_____

_____

b. Relate Cause and Effect What causes wind to deposit sand or other sediment?

_____

_____

c. CHALLENGE In a desert, a soil mixture of sand and small rocks is exposed to wind erosion. How would the land surface change over time?

_____

_____

_____

_____

got it? ....

O **I get it!** Now I know that wind causes erosion through _____

O I need extra help with _____

Go to **MY SCIENCE** 🄢 **COACH** online for help with this subject.

3 Study Guide

The surface of the land is shaped by the processes of erosion and deposition caused by gravity, _____, _____, glaciers, and _____.

LESSON 1 Mass Movement

🔑 Weathering, erosion, and deposition act together in a cycle that wears down and builds up Earth's surface.

🔑 The different types of mass movement include landslides, mudflows, slumps, and creep.

Vocabulary
- erosion • sediment • deposition
- gravity • mass movement

LESSON 2 Water Erosion

🔑 Moving water is the major agent of erosion that has shaped Earth's land surface. Groundwater erodes through chemical weathering.

🔑 Through erosion, a river forms valleys, waterfalls, flood plains, meanders, and oxbow lakes. Deposition forms alluvial fans and deltas.

Vocabulary
- runoff • rill • gully • stream • tributary
- flood plain • meander • oxbow lake
- delta • alluvial fan • groundwater
- stalactite • stalagmite • karst topography

LESSON 3 Glacial Erosion

🔑 Glaciers can form only in an area where more snow falls than melts.

🔑 Continental glaciers can flow in all directions as they move.

🔑 Gravity constantly pulls a glacier downhill.

🔑 Glaciers erode the land through plucking and abrasion. When a glacier melts, it deposits the sediment it eroded from the land.

Vocabulary
- glacier • continental glacier • ice age
- valley glacier • plucking • till • moraine • kettle

LESSON 4 Wave Erosion

🔑 Waves shape the coast through erosion by breaking down rock and moving sand and other sediment.

🔑 Waves shape a coast when they deposit sediment, forming coastal features such as beaches, sandbars, barrier beaches, and spits.

Vocabulary
- headland • beach
- longshore drift • spit

LESSON 5 Wind Erosion

🔑 Wind erosion and deposition may form sand dunes and loess deposits.

Vocabulary
- deflation
- sand dune
- loess

Review and Assessment

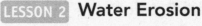

LESSON 1 Mass Movement

1. What is the process by which weathered rock, sediment, and soil are moved from place to place?

    a. runoff   **b.** delta formation

    c. erosion   **d.** longshore drift

2. Freezing and thawing of water can cause creep, which is _____

_____

3. Compare and Contrast How are landslides and mudflows similar? How are they different?

_____

_____

_____

_____

4. Sequence Identify the steps in the erosion cycle. Explain why it has no beginning or end.

_____

_____

_____

_____

_____

_____

5. Relate Cause and Effect What type of mass movement is shown below? Explain.

_____

_____

LESSON 2 Water Erosion

6. Which feature typically contains water only during a rainstorm and right after it rains?

    a. a river   **b.** a rill

    c. a gully   **d.** a stream

7. Sediments are deposited in an alluvial fan

because _____

_____

8. Sequence Complete the flowchart about stream formation.

Stream Formation

Raindrops strike ground.

↓

Runoff forms.

↓

a. _____

↓

b. _____

↓

c. _____

↓

d. _____

9. Make Judgments Your family looks at a new house right on a riverbank. Why might they hesitate to buy this house?

_____

_____

_____

_____

10. Write About It Explain to visitors to your valley how the lake called *Oxbow Lake* formed. Use words and a drawing.

Glacial Erosion

11. What do you call a mass of rock and soil deposited directly by a glacier?

   a. kettle   **b.** till

   c. slump   **d.** loess

12. When glaciers drag attached rocks across the

   land, they _____

   _____

13. Solve Problems You're in the mountains studying a valley glacier. What methods would you use to tell if it is advancing or retreating?

   _____

   _____

   _____

   _____

   _____

 Wave Erosion

14. What is a rocky part of the shore that sticks out in the ocean?

   a. spit   **b.** barrier beach

   c. rill   **d.** headland

15. Waves change direction as they near shore

   because _____

   _____

16. Apply Concepts Under what conditions would you expect abrasion to cause the most erosion on a beach?

   _____

   _____

17. Write About It You're walking on a beach and see a spit. Explain how a spit could have formed from a rocky headland.

 Wind Erosion

18. What do you call the erosion of sediment by wind?

   a. drifting   **b.** deposition

   c. plucking   **d.** deflation

19. Compare and Contrast How is wind deflation different from wind abrasion?

   _____

   _____

   _____

   _____

   _____

20. Relate Cause and Effect How does a loess deposit form?

   _____

   _____

   _____

What processes shape the surface of the land?

21. Suppose you are a geologist traveling in a region that has limestone bedrock and plenty of rainfall. What features would you expect to find in this landscape? How do they form?

   _____

   _____

   _____

   _____

   _____

   _____

   _____

   _____

   _____

Standardized Test Prep

Multiple Choice

Circle the letter of the best answer.

1. The diagram shows a meander. Where would sediment likely be eroded to help form an oxbow?

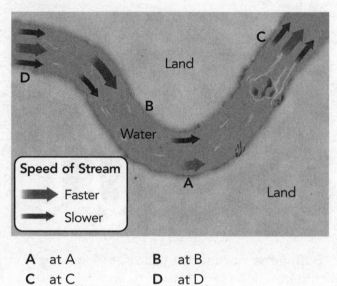

Speed of Stream
➡ Faster
➡ Slower

A at A	**B** at B
C at C	**D** at D

2. What is the slow, downhill mass movement of rock and soil caused by gravity?

A creep	**B** a glacier
C a landslide	**D** runoff

3. What is an alluvial fan?

   A a landform created by wind deposition
   B a landform created by water erosion
   C a landform created by glacial erosion
   D a landform created by water deposition

4. What is the name for a small depression created by the melting of a chunk of ice in glacial sediment?

A till	**B** kettle
C moraine	**D** spit

5. What "drifts" in longshore drift?

A a chunk of glacier	**B** a river's course
C beach sediment	**D** groundwater

Constructed Response

Use the diagram below and your knowledge of science to help you answer Question 6. Write your answer on a separate piece of paper.

6. Describe how gravity affects the erosion of Earth's surface in mass movement, running water, and glaciers.

Floodwater Fallout

In June 2008, large portions of Illinois, Indiana, Iowa, Michigan, Minnesota, Missouri, and Wisconsin were under water. Weeks of rain and spring melting caused rivers in these states to overflow their banks and flood the surrounding flood plains. Where water broke through levees, families were evacuated, roads closed, and several counties were declared disaster zones. Farmland, homes, and businesses located on flood plains suffered billions of dollars' worth of damage.

We can't control the weather. When melting snow and heavy rains cause rivers to flood, some of the water may overflow onto undeveloped riverbanks and wetlands. In these places, the soil absorbs some of the water, and trees and other plants often survive the damage. But when rivers flood houses, streets, and businesses, the water can't drain. It destroys homes and businesses, causing huge amounts of damage.

At least ten million households in the United States are located on flood plains. Levees and dams protect some communities. In others, public officials make laws to prevent building on flood plains. To encourage communities to take action, the government offers flood insurance for cities and towns that take steps to reduce flood damage. We cannot stop the rain from falling or the rivers from flooding, but we can take new approaches to reduce the damage.

Communicate It Find out if your community is located on a flood plain. If you do not live near a flood plain, learn about a community that is on one. Research what plans exist for helping people during and after a flood. Suppose developers want to build homes on the flood plains in your community. What problems might this cause? What benefits might the new development bring? Write a letter to a public official giving your opinion. Support your opinion with facts from your research.

Any Way the Wind Blows

Mars is a pretty cool place. Gusts of wind blow frosty sand dunes around and cause strange streaks of sand and frost. When the Mars Rovers arrived on Mars in 2004, scientists at the National Aeronautics and Space Administration got their first chance to learn about wind and erosion on another planet. The rovers captured pictures of grains of Martian sand (called "blueberries" by the scientists) and of the patterns of dust and rock on the surface of Mars. From these pictures, scientists learned a lot about wind erosion.

By measuring these Martian blueberries and recording where they landed on the surface, scientists could estimate how strong Martian winds must be. Looking at the patterns of sand and bare rock, they could tell which directions the winds on Mars blow. Data showed that they blow from either the northwest or the southeast.

Scientists used all their measuring, counting, and other observations to design a computer model. The model can describe what happens to a planet's sandy surface when the wind starts blowing. By counting millions of blueberries on Mars, scientists are learning how to track wind erosion anywhere in the solar system!

Research It Dr. Douglas Jerolmack is a geophysicist who helped prove there is wind on Mars. Research Dr. Jerolmack's observations. Write a paragraph giving reasons why Dr. Jerolmack's scientific claims are considered to be valid (true).

▲ Scientists measured "blueberries"—grains of Martian sand and dust.

WHAT CAN YOU LEARN FROM A BUG?

How do scientists study Earth's past?

Long ago, a fly got stuck in resin from a tree. Today, that fly is a fossil that scientists can study. It's a clue to what Earth was like on the day the fly got stuck. **Develop Hypotheses** **What do you think scientists can learn from fossils like this?**

_____
_____
_____
_____
_____
_____
_____
_____

> **UNTAMED SCIENCE** Watch the **Untamed Science** video to learn more about fossils.

A Trip Through Geologic Time

4 Getting Started

Check Your Understanding

1. Background Read the paragraph below and then answer the question.

Forces inside Earth move large pieces, or plates, of Earth's crust very slowly over long periods of time. These forces are explained by plate tectonics. Where these plates meet, volcanic eruptions can produce igneous rocks. Over time, rivers, wind, and ice can break down the rocks and carry sediment to new places.

The theory of **plate tectonics** states that pieces of Earth's upper layers move slowly, carried by convection currents inside Earth.

An **igneous rock** forms when melted material hardens inside Earth or on the surface.

Sediment is made up of small pieces of rock and other material.

• How do volcanic eruptions produce rocks?

_____

_____

> **MY READING WEB** If you had trouble answering the question above, visit **My Reading Web** and type in *A Trip Through Geologic Time.*

Vocabulary Skill

Prefixes The root of a word is the part of the word that carries the basic meaning. A prefix is a word part placed in front of the root to change the meaning of the root or to form a new word. Look at the examples in the table below.

Prefix	Meaning	Example
in-	inside, inward	intrusion, *n.*
ex-	outside, outward	extrusion, *n.*
super-	over, above	superposition, *n.*

2. Quick Check The root *–trusion* means "pushing." What might *extrusion* mean?_____

fossil

intrusion

law of superposition

vertebrate

Chapter Preview

LESSON 1
- fossil • mold • cast
- petrified fossil • carbon film
- trace fossil • paleontologist
- evolution • extinct

↻ **Compare and Contrast**
△ **Pose Questions**

LESSON 2
- relative age • absolute age
- law of superposition • extrusion
- intrusion • fault • index fossil
- unconformity

↻ **Relate Text and Visuals**
△ **Infer**

LESSON 3
- radioactive decay • half-life

↻ **Identify the Main Idea**
△ **Calculate**

LESSON 4
- geologic time scale • era
- period

↻ **Summarize**
△ **Make Models**

LESSON 5
- comet

↻ **Sequence**
△ **Communicate**

LESSON 6
- invertebrate • vertebrate
- amphibian • reptile
- mass extinction • mammal

↻ **Identify Supporting Evidence**
△ **Classify**

▸ **VOCAB FLASH CARDS** For extra help with vocabulary, visit **Vocab Flash Cards** and type in *A Trip Through Geologic Time.*

1 Fossils

UNLOCK THE BIG Q?

🔑 **What Are Fossils?**

🔑 **What Are the Kinds of Fossils?**

🔑 **What Do Fossils Show?**

my PLANET DiARY

DISCOVERY

A Dinosaur Named Sue

On a hot day in August 1990, Sue Hendrickson was hunting for fossils near the town of Faith, South Dakota. She found some little pieces of bone below a cliff. When she looked up at the cliff, she saw more bones. These bones weren't little. They were enormous! She and other scientists determined that they were the bones of a *Tyrannosaurus rex*. In fact, she'd found the largest and most complete skeleton of a *Tyrannosaurus* ever discovered. Today, the skeleton, nicknamed "Sue," is on display at the Field Museum in Chicago.

✏️ **Communicate** Write your answer to each question below. Then discuss your answers with a partner.

1. What science skills did Sue Hendrickson use when she discovered Sue?

_____

_____

2. What do you think scientists can learn by studying dinosaur skeletons?

_____

_____

_____

▶ PLANET DIARY Go to **Planet Diary** to learn more about fossils.

Lab zone® Do the Inquiry Warm-Up *What's in a Rock?*

Vocabulary

- fossil • mold • cast • petrified fossil • carbon film
- trace fossil • paleontologist • evolution • extinct

Skills

↻ **Reading:** Compare and Contrast

△ **Inquiry:** Pose Questions

What Are Fossils?

Sue is one of the most nearly complete dinosaur fossils ever found. **Fossils** are the preserved remains or traces of living things. 🔑 **Most fossils form when living things die and are buried by sediment. The sediment slowly hardens into rock and preserves the shapes of the organisms.** Sediment is made up of rock particles or the remains of living things. Most fossils form from animals or plants that once lived in or near quiet water such as swamps, lakes, or shallow seas where sediment builds up. In **Figure 1,** you can see how a fossil might form.

When an organism dies, its soft parts often decay quickly or are eaten by animals. That is why only hard parts of an organism generally leave fossils. These hard parts include bones, shells, teeth, seeds, and woody stems. It is rare for the soft parts of an organism to become a fossil.

FIGURE 1 ·······························

▷ **INTERACTIVE ART** **How a Fossil Forms**

A fossil may form when sediment quickly covers an organism's body.

An organism dies and sinks to the bottom of a lake.

The organism is covered by sediment.

✎ **Sequence** What happens next?

_____

_____

Lab zone ®   Do the Quick Lab *Sweet Fossils.*

🔑 Assess Your Understanding

got it? ···

○ **I get it!** Now I know that fossils are_____

_____

○ **I need extra help with** _____

Go to **my science** ⑤ **COACH** *online for help with this subject.*

What Are the Kinds of Fossils?

Fossils found in rock include molds and casts, petrified fossils, carbon films, and trace fossils. Other fossils form when the remains of organisms are preserved in substances such as tar, amber, or ice. Look at examples of the kinds of fossils in **Figure 2**.

Molds and Casts The most common fossils are molds and casts. A **mold** is a hollow area in sediment in the shape of an organism or part of an organism. A mold forms when the organism is buried in sediment. Later, water may deposit minerals and sediment into a mold, forming a cast. A **cast** is a solid copy of the shape of an organism. Molds and casts can preserve fine details.

Petrified Fossils A fossil may form when the remains of an organism become petrified. The term *petrified* means "turned into stone." **Petrified fossils** are fossils in which minerals replace all of an organism, or a part, such as a dinosaur bone. This can also happen to wood, such as tree trunks. Water carrying minerals seeps into spaces in the plant's cells. Over time, the water evaporates, leaving the minerals behind.

Carbon Films Another type of fossil is a **carbon film,** an extremely thin coating of carbon on rock. When sediment buries an organism, some gases escape from the sediment, leaving carbon behind. Eventually, only a thin film of carbon remains. This process can preserve the delicate parts of plant leaves and insects.

Compare and Contrast How are carbon films and preserved remains different?

_____

_____

_____

_____

_____

_____

FIGURE 2 ························
Types of Fossils
In addition to petrified fossils, fossils may be molds and casts, carbon films, trace fossils, or preserved remains.

✎ **Classify** Identify each fossil shown here by its type.

Raised Fern
This fossil shows the texture of a leaf. Fossil type:

_____

Fine Details
This fossil preserves a thin layer that shows the details of an ancient insect. Fossil type:

_____

Hollow Fern
Can you see the veins in this plant leaf? Fossil type:

_____

Where They Walked
This footprint shows how a dinosaur walked. Fossil type:

_____

apply it!

This fossil is of an ancient organism called *Archaeopteryx*. Study the photograph and then answer the questions.

1 What type of fossil is this?

_____

2 🔺 **Pose Questions** List two questions about the organism that studying this fossil could help you answer.

_____

_____

Trace Fossils

Trace fossils provide evidence of the activities of ancient organisms. A fossilized footprint is one example. In such a fossil, a print is buried by sediment, which slowly becomes solid rock. Trails and burrows can also become trace fossils.

Preserved Remains

Some processes can preserve entire organisms. For example, some organisms become trapped in sticky tar or tree resin. When the resin hardens, it becomes a substance called amber. Freezing can also preserve remains.

Frozen in Time
Ice preserved even the fur and skin of this woolly mammoth for thousands of years. Fossil type:

_____

From Wood to Stone
Minerals replaced other materials inside this tree, producing the colors shown here. Fossil type:

_____

Lab zone ® Do the Quick Lab *Modeling Trace Fossils.*

🔲 Assess Your Understanding

1a. Identify A (mold/trace fossil) can form when sediment buries the hard part of an organism.

b. Explain A petrified fossil forms when

_____ replace parts of

a(n) _____ .

c. Make Generalizations What might you learn from a carbon film that you could not learn from a cast?

_____

_____

got it? ●●●

○ **I get it!** Now I know that the kinds of fossils are _____

_____

_____

○ **I need extra help with** _____

Go to **MY SCIENCE** ⑤ **COACH** online for help with this subject.

What Do Fossils Show?

Would you like to hunt for fossils all over the world? And what could you learn from them? Scientists who study fossils are called **paleontologists** (pay lee un TAHL uh jists). Together, all the information that paleontologists have gathered about past life is called the fossil record. 🔑 **The fossil record provides evidence about the history of life and past environments on Earth. The fossil record also shows how different groups of organisms have changed over time.**

Fossils and Past Environments Paleontologists use fossils to build up a picture of Earth's past environments. The fossils found in an area tell whether the area was a shallow bay, an ocean bottom, or a freshwater swamp.

Fossils also provide evidence about the past climate of a region. For example, coal has been found in Antarctica. But coal forms only from the remains of plants that grow in warm, swampy regions. The presence of coal shows that the climate of Antarctica was once much warmer than it is today. **Figure 3** shows another example of how fossils show change in an environment.

FIGURE 3 ·······················

> INTERACTIVE ART **Wyoming, 50 Million Years Ago**
Today, as you can see in the postcard, Wyoming has areas of dry plateaus. But 50 million years ago, the area was very different. ✎ **Infer** Identify the organism or kind of organism shown by fossils a, b, and c.

Palms

a

b

c

Crocodilian

Bat

CHALLENGE What features of *Hyracotherium* show that it is related to horses?

_____

_____

_____

_____

Gar

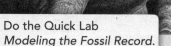

Change and the Fossil Record The fossil record also reveals changes in organisms. Older rocks contain fossils of simpler organisms. Younger rocks contain fossils of both simple and more complex organisms. In other words, the fossil record shows that life on Earth has evolved, or changed over time. **Evolution** is the change in living things over time.

The fossil record shows that millions of types of organisms have evolved. But many others, including the dinosaurs, have become extinct. A type of organism is **extinct** if it no longer exists and will never again live on Earth.

Scientists use fossils to reconstruct extinct organisms and determine how they may be related to living organisms. For example, the animals called *Hyracotherium* in **Figure 3** are related to modern horses.

Sequoia

Uintatherium

Hyracotherium

Coryphodon

Greetings FROM WYOMING

Lab zone Do the Quick Lab
Modeling the Fossil Record.

🔑 Assess Your Understanding

2a. Explain What does the fossil record show about how life has changed over time?

_____

_____

_____

b. Apply Concepts Give an example of a question you could ask about a fossil of an extinct organism.

_____

_____

_____

got it? •••••••••••••••••••••••••••••••••••

○ **I get it!** Now I know that the fossil record

shows _____

_____

_____

○ **I need extra help with** _____

Go to MY SCIENCE ⓢ COACH *online for help with this subject.*

The Relative Age of Rocks

UNLOCK
THE BIG
?

🔑 How Old Are Rock Layers?

🔑 How Can Rock Layers Change?

my planet diary

BLOG

Posted by Owen

Location Tacoma, WA

A couple of summers ago, my dad took me rock climbing for the first time. I went to a place called Frenchman Coulee in central Washington. It was really cool because the rock was basalt, which forms in giant pillars. It starts as lava, and then cools and you can see the different lava flows in the rock. Another cool thing is that Frenchman Coulee, which is a canyon, was gouged out by huge Ice Age floods.

✏️ Communicate Discuss the question below with a partner. Then answer it on your own.

How do you think scientists figure out the age of the basalt layers at Frenchman Coulee?

_____

_____

_____

_____

> PLANET DIARY Go to Planet Diary to learn more about the age of rock layers.

Lab zone Do the Inquiry Warm-Up
Which Layer Is the Oldest?

How Old Are Rock Layers?

If you found a fossil in a rock, you might start by asking, "What is it?" Your next question would probably be, "How old is it?" The first step is to find the age of the rock.

Relative and Absolute Age Geologists have two ways to express the age of a rock. The **relative age** of a rock is its age compared to the ages of other rocks. You have probably used the idea of relative age when comparing your age with someone else's. For example, if you say that you are older than your brother but younger than your sister, you are describing your relative age.

Vocabulary

- relative age • absolute age • law of superposition
- extrusion • intrusion • fault • index fossil
- unconformity

Skills

- Reading: Relate Text and Visuals
- Inquiry: Infer

The relative age of a rock does not provide its absolute age. The **absolute age** of a rock is the number of years that have passed since the rock formed. It may be impossible to know a rock's absolute age exactly, so geologists often use both absolute and relative ages.

Rock Layers Fossils are most often found in layers of sedimentary rock. Geologists use the **law of superposition** to determine the relative ages of sedimentary rock layers. **According to the law of superposition, in undisturbed horizontal sedimentary rock layers the oldest layer is at the bottom. Each higher layer is younger than the layers below it.** The deeper you go, the older the rocks are.

Figure 1 shows rock layers in the Grand Canyon. Rock layers like these form a record of Earth's history. Scientists can study this record to understand how Earth and life on Earth have changed.

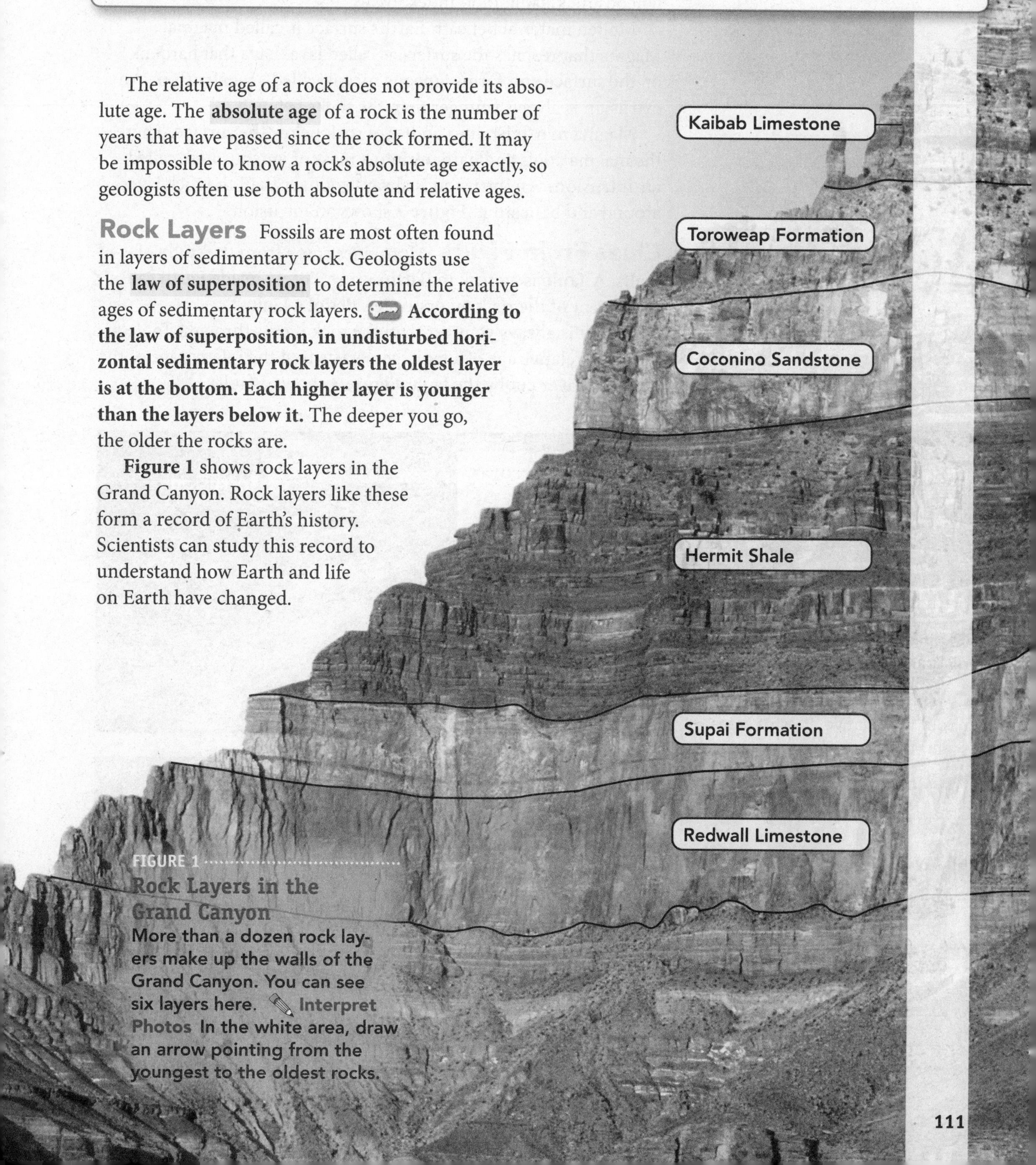

Kaibab Limestone

Toroweap Formation

Coconino Sandstone

Hermit Shale

Supai Formation

Redwall Limestone

FIGURE 1

Rock Layers in the Grand Canyon

More than a dozen rock layers make up the walls of the Grand Canyon. You can see six layers here. ✎ Interpret Photos In the white area, draw an arrow pointing from the youngest to the oldest rocks.

Vocabulary Prefixes How does knowing the prefixes *in-* and *ex-* help you remember the difference between an intrusion and an extrusion?

_____

_____

_____

_____

_____

_____

Clues From Igneous Rock

There are other clues to the relative ages of rocks besides the position of rock layers. To determine relative age, geologists also study extrusions and intrusions of igneous rock, faults, and index fossils.

Molten material beneath Earth's surface is called magma. Magma that reaches the surface is called lava. Lava that hardens on the surface and forms igneous rock is called an **extrusion.** An extrusion is always younger than the rocks below it.

Magma may push into bodies of rock below the surface. There, the magma cools and hardens into a mass of igneous rock called an **intrusion.** An intrusion is always younger than the rock layers around and beneath it. **Figure 2** shows an intrusion.

Clues From Faults

More clues come from the study of faults. A **fault** is a break in Earth's crust. Forces inside Earth cause movement of the rock on opposite sides of a fault.

A fault is always younger than the rock it cuts through. To determine the relative age of a fault, geologists find the relative age of the youngest layer cut by the fault. **Figure 3** shows a fault.

apply it!

The diagram below shows rock layers found at a site.

1 Circle the area on the diagram that shows an intrusion.

2 Shade the oldest layer on the diagram.

3 Infer What can you infer about the relative ages of areas B and E?

_____

_____

_____

_____

_____

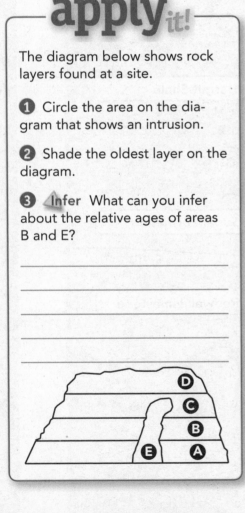

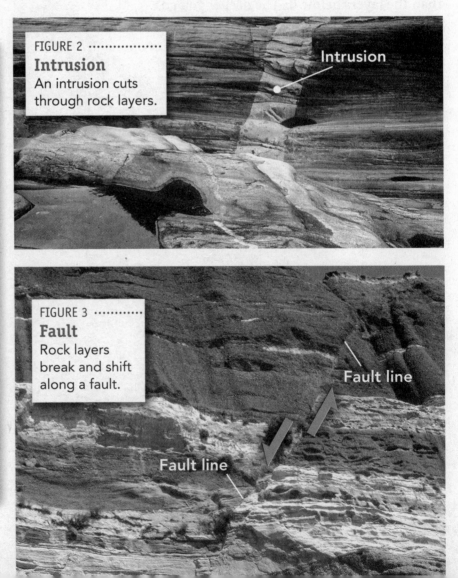

FIGURE 2 ·················
Intrusion
An intrusion cuts through rock layers.

Intrusion

FIGURE 3 ············
Fault
Rock layers break and shift along a fault.

Fault line

Fault line

How Do Fossils Show Age?

To date rock layers, geologists first find the relative age of a layer of rock at one location. Then they can match layers in other locations to that layer.

Certain fossils, called index fossils, help geologists match rock layers. To be useful as an **index fossil,** a fossil must be widely distributed and represent an organism that existed for a geologically short period of time. 🔑 **Index fossils are useful because they tell the relative ages of the rock layers in which they occur.** Scientists infer that layers with matching index fossils are the same age.

You can use index fossils to match rock layers. Look at **Figure 4,** which shows rock layers from four different locations. Notice that two of the fossils are found in only one of these rock layers. These are the index fossils.

FIGURE 4 ·······················
> **INTERACTIVE ART** Index Fossils

Scientists use index fossils to match rock layers.

✏️ **Interpret Diagrams** Label the layers to match the first area shown. Circle the fossil or fossils that you can use as index fossils. What can you infer about the history of Location 4?

_____

_____

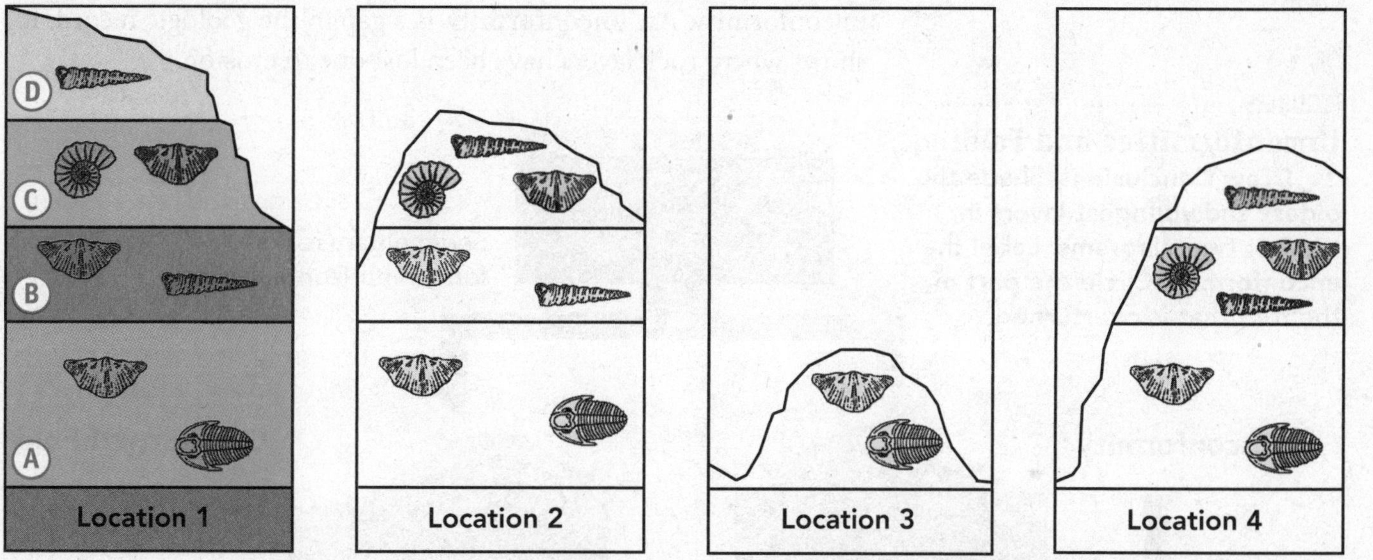

| Location 1 | Location 2 | Location 3 | Location 4 |

Do the Lab Investigation
Exploring Geologic Time Through Core Samples.

🔑 **Assess Your Understanding**

1a. Explain In an area with several different rock layers, which is oldest? Explain.

_____

_____

_____

b. Infer How could a geologist match the rock layers in one area to rock layers found in another area?

_____

_____

_____

_____

got it? ···

○ **I get it!** Now I know that you can find the relative age of rocks by_____

_____

○ **I need extra help with**_____

Go to MY SCIENCE COACH online for help with this subject.

How Can Rock Layers Change?

The geologic record of sedimentary rock layers is not complete. In fact, most of Earth's geologic record has been lost to erosion. 🔑 **Gaps in the geologic record and folding can change the position in which rock layers appear.** Motion along faults can also change how rock layers line up. These changes make it harder for scientists to reconstruct Earth's history. **Figure 5** shows how the order of rock layers may change.

Gaps in the Geologic Record When rock layers erode away, an older rock surface may be exposed. Then deposition begins again, building new rock layers. The surface where new rock layers meet a much older rock surface beneath them is called an unconformity. An **unconformity** is a gap in the geologic record. It shows where rock layers have been lost due to erosion.

✏️ **Relate Text and Visuals**
Underline the sentences that explain how the rock layers in **Figure 5** changed.

FIGURE 5 ·······························

Unconformities and Folding
✏️ **Draw Conclusions** Shade the oldest and youngest layers in the last two diagrams. Label the unconformity. Circle the part of the fold that is overturned.

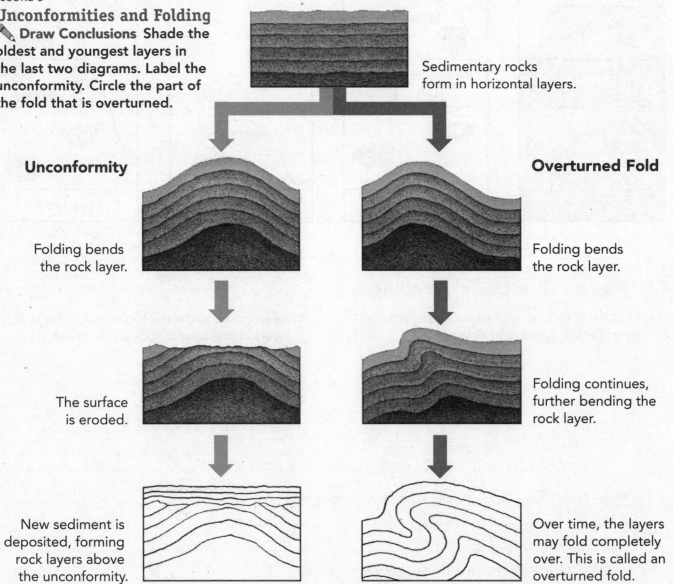

Sedimentary rocks form in horizontal layers.

Unconformity

Folding bends the rock layer.

The surface is eroded.

New sediment is deposited, forming rock layers above the unconformity.

Overturned Fold

Folding bends the rock layer.

Folding continues, further bending the rock layer.

Over time, the layers may fold completely over. This is called an overturned fold.

Folding Sometimes, forces inside Earth fold rock layers so much that the layers are turned over completely. In this case, the youngest rock layers may be on the bottom!

No one place holds a complete geologic record. Geologists compare rock layers in many places to piece together as complete a sequence as possible.

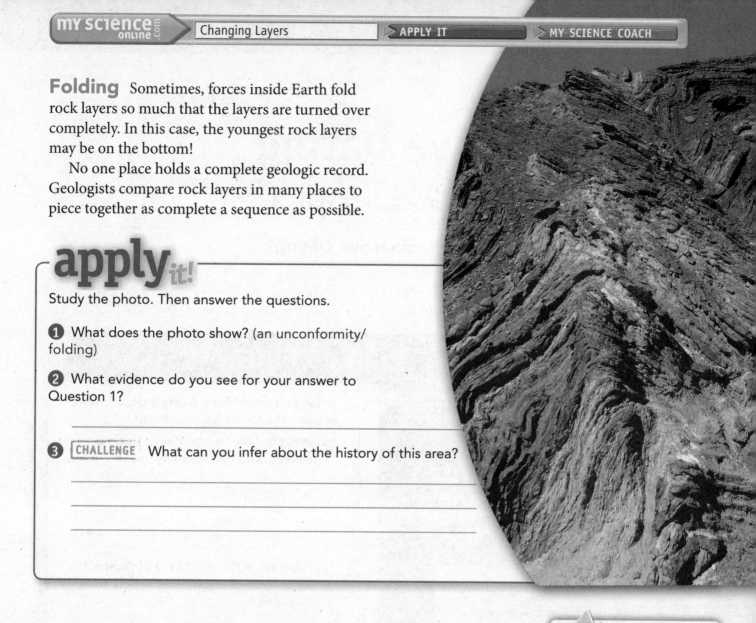

apply it!

Study the photo. Then answer the questions.

1 What does the photo show? (an unconformity/ folding)

2 What evidence do you see for your answer to Question 1?

_____

3 CHALLENGE What can you infer about the history of this area?

_____

_____

_____

Lab zone® Do the Quick Lab *How Did It Form?*

🔑 Assess Your Understanding

2a. List Name two ways rock layers can change.

_____

b. Explain How does folding change rock layers?

_____

_____

_____

c. Draw Conclusions Two locations include a layer of rock with a particular index fossil. In one location, the layer occurs in a higher position than in the other. What can you conclude about the history of the two areas?

_____

_____

_____

got it? ....

○ **I get it!** Now I know that rock layers can change due to _____

_____

○ **I need extra help with**_____

Go to my science ⑤ coacн *online for help with this subject.*

115

Radioactive Dating

🔑 **What Is Radioactive Decay?**

🔑 **What Is Radioactive Dating?**

my planet Diary

VOICES FROM HISTORY

Marie Curie

In 1896, French scientists named Marie and Pierre Curie heard about experiments that had been done by another scientist, Henri Becquerel (bek uh REL). Marie Curie later described what happened:

Becquerel had shown that by placing some uranium salt on a photographic plate, covered with black paper, the plate would be affected as if light had fallen on it. The effect is produced by special rays which are emitted by the uranium salt.... My determinations showed that the emission of the rays is an atomic property of the uranium.

The property that Becquerel and the Curies discovered was called radioactivity. Today, radioactivity is used for many purposes—including finding the age of rocks!

After you read Marie Curie's description, answer the following questions.

1. What did Marie and Pierre Curie discover about radioactivity?

_____

_____

_____

2. What does the discovery of radioactivity tell you about how scientists work together?

_____

_____

_____

> **PLANET DIARY** Go to **Planet Diary** to learn more about the uses of radioactivity.

Lab zone® Do the Inquiry Warm-Up *How Long Till It's Gone?*

Vocabulary
- radioactive decay
- half-life

Skills
- ↪ Reading: Identify the Main Idea
- △ Inquiry: Calculate

What Is Radioactive Decay?

Most elements usually do not change. But some elements can break down, or decay, over time. These elements release particles and energy in a process called **radioactive decay.** These elements are said to be radioactive. ◠ **During radioactive decay, the atoms of one element break down to form atoms of another element.**

Half-Life The rate of decay of each radioactive element never changes. The **half-life** of a radioactive element is the time it takes for half of the radioactive atoms to decay. You can see in **Figure 1** how a radioactive element decays over time.

FIGURE 1 ···

Half-Life
The half-life of a radioactive element is the amount of time it takes for half of the radioactive atoms to decay.

✎ **Graph** What pattern do you see in the graph? Use the pattern to complete the last bar.

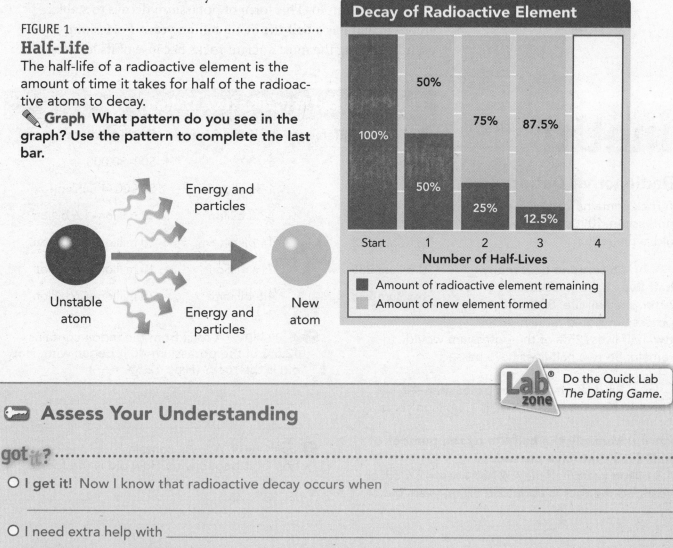

Decay of Radioactive Element

100% — 50% — 75% — 87.5%

50% — 25% — 12.5%

Start — 1 — 2 — 3 — 4
Number of Half-Lives

■ Amount of radioactive element remaining
▢ Amount of new element formed

Unstable atom → Energy and particles → New atom
Energy and particles

Lab zone® Do the Quick Lab *The Dating Game.*

◠ Assess Your Understanding

got it? ··

○ **I get it!** Now I know that radioactive decay occurs when _____

○ **I need extra help with** _____

Go to my science ☁ coach *online for help with this subject.*

What Is Radioactive Dating?

Radioactive elements occur naturally in igneous rocks. Scientists use the rate at which these elements decay to calculate the rock's age. As a radioactive element within the igneous rock decays, it changes into another element. So the composition of the rock changes slowly over time. The amount of the radioactive element decreases. But the amount of the new element increases.

Determining Absolute Ages Geologists use radioactive dating to determine the absolute ages of rocks. 🗝 **In radioactive dating, scientists first determine the amount of a radioactive element in a rock. Then they compare that amount with the amount of the stable element into which the radioactive element decays.** They use this information and the half-life of the element to calculate the age of the rock.

Potassium-Argon Dating Scientists often date rocks using potassium-40. This form of potassium decays to stable argon-40 and has a half-life of 1.3 billion years. Potassium-40 is useful in dating the most ancient rocks because of its long half-life.

do the math!

Radioactive Dating

A rock contains 25% of the potassium-40 it started with. How old is the rock?

STEP ① Determine how many half-lives have passed.
After one half-life, 50% of the potassium would remain. After two half-lives, 25% of the potassium would remain. So two half-lives have passed.

STEP ② Find the half-life of potassium-40.
The half-life of potassium-40 is 1.3 billion years.

STEP ③ Multiply the half-life by the number of half-lives that have passed.
1.3 billion years/half-life × 2 half-lives = 2.6 billion years, so the rock is about 2.6 billion years old.

Elements Used in Radioactive Dating

Radioactive Element	Half-life (years)	Dating Range (years)
Carbon-14	5,730	500–50,000
Potassium-40	1.3 billion	50,000–4.6 billion
Rubidium-87	48.8 billion	10 million–4.6 billion
Thorium-232	14 billion	10 million–4.6 billion
Uranium-235	713 million	10 million–4.6 billion
Uranium-238	4.5 billion	10 million–4.6 billion

❶ **Calculate** A rock from the moon contains 12.5% of the potassium-40 it began with. How old is the rock? (*Hint:* 12.5% = $\frac{1}{8}$)

_____

_____

❷ **Calculate** A fossil contains $\frac{1}{16}$ of the carbon-14 it began with. How old is the fossil?

_____

_____

Carbon-14 Dating

Carbon-14 is a radioactive form of carbon. All plants and animals contain carbon, including some carbon-14. After an organism dies, the carbon-14 in the organism's body decays. It changes to stable nitrogen-14. To determine the age of a sample, scientists measure the amount of carbon-14 that is left in the organism's remains. Carbon-14 has been used to date fossils such as frozen mammoths and the skeletons of prehistoric humans.

Carbon-14 has a half-life of only 5,730 years. For this reason, it generally can't be used to date fossils or rocks older than about 50,000 years. The amount of carbon-14 left would be too small to measure accurately. Also, most rocks do not contain much carbon.

Identify the Main Idea
Underline the main idea in the first paragraph to the left.

FIGURE 2 ....

REAL-WORLD INQUIRY Using Carbon-14 Dating
Scientists have dated these skeletons to 5,000–6,000 years ago. But they do not use radioactive dating to find the age of stone artifacts made by people.
✎ **Make Generalizations** Why not?

_____

_____

_____

_____

Lab zone Do the Quick Lab *How Old Is It?*

🔑 Assess Your Understanding

1a. Identify Scientists use the method of (radioactive dating/relative dating) to find the absolute age of a rock.

b. Apply Concepts The half-life of thorium-232 is 14 billion years. A rock with 25% of its thorium-232 remaining is _____ years old.

c. **CHALLENGE** A scientist finds stone tools in the ruins of an ancient house. The house also has ashes in a fireplace. How could the scientist estimate the age of the stone tools?

_____

_____

_____

_____

got it? ....

○ **I get it!** Now I know that radioactive dating is done by _____

_____

○ **I need extra help with** _____

Go to **my science** 🔍 **COACH** online for help with this subject.

4 The Geologic Time Scale

UNLOCK THE BIG ?

🔑 **What Is the Geologic Time Scale?**

my planeT DiaRY

SCIENCE STATS

Earth's History in a Day

Suppose you could squeeze all of Earth's 4.6-billion-year history into one 24-hour day. The table shows the times at which some major events would take place.

	Time	First Appearance
A	Midnight	Earth
B	3:00 A.M.	Rocks
C	4:00 A.M.	Bacteria
D	2:00 P.M.	Algae
E	8:30–9:00 P.M.	Seaweeds and jellyfish
F	10:00 P.M.	Land plants
G	10:50 P.M.	Dinosaurs
H	11:39 P.M.	Mammals
I	11:58:43 P.M.	Humans

Use the data in the table to answer these questions.

1. ✏️ **Sequence** Write the letter for each event on the clock diagram.

2. Did anything surprise you about the data? If so, what?

_____

_____

▷ PLANET DIARY Go to **Planet Diary** to learn more about Earth's history.

Lab zone® Do the Inquiry Warm-Up *This Is Your Life!*

Vocabulary
- geologic time scale
- era • period

Skills
- Reading: Summarize
- Inquiry; Make Models

What Is the Geologic Time Scale?

When you speak of the past, what names do you use for different spans of time? You probably use names such as century, decade, year, month, week, and day. But these units aren't very helpful for thinking about much longer periods of time. Scientists needed to develop a way to talk about Earth's history.

Because the time span of Earth's past is so great, geologists use the geologic time scale to show Earth's history. The geologic time scale is a record of the geologic events and the evolution of life forms as shown in the fossil record.

Scientists first developed the geologic time scale by studying rock layers and index fossils worldwide. With this information, scientists placed Earth's rocks in order by relative age. Later, radioactive dating helped determine the absolute age of the divisions in the geologic time scale. **Figure 1** shows some of the earliest known rocks.

FIGURE 1 ·······

Ancient Rocks

The Isua rocks in Greenland are among the oldest rocks on Earth. They formed after heat and pressure changed sedimentary rocks that formed under early oceans.

Summarize Write two or three sentences to summarize the information on this page.

_____

_____

_____

_____

_____

_____

FIGURE 2 ·······················

The Geologic Time Scale

The divisions of the geologic time scale are used to date events in Earth's history.

✎ **Calculate** After you read the next page, calculate and fill in the duration of each period. Then use the time scale to identify the period in which each organism below lived.

Organism: *Wiwaxia*
Age: about 500 million years
Period: _____

Organism: *Velociraptor*
Age: about 80 million years
Period: _____

Organism: *Smilodon*
Age: about 12,000 years
Period: _____

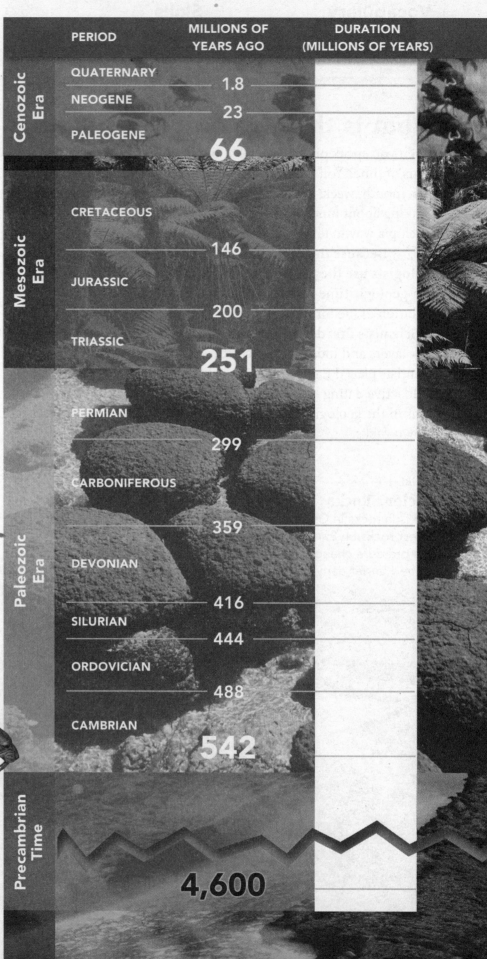

	PERIOD	MILLIONS OF YEARS AGO	DURATION (MILLIONS OF YEARS)
Cenozoic Era	QUATERNARY		
		1.8	
	NEOGENE		
		23	
	PALEOGENE		
		66	
Mesozoic Era	CRETACEOUS		
		146	
	JURASSIC		
		200	
	TRIASSIC		
		251	
Paleozoic Era	PERMIAN		
		299	
	CARBONIFEROUS		
		359	
	DEVONIAN		
		416	
	SILURIAN		
		444	
	ORDOVICIAN		
		488	
	CAMBRIAN		
		542	
Precambrian Time			
		4,600	

Dividing Geologic Time As geologists studied the fossil record, they found major changes in life forms at certain times. They used these changes to mark where one unit of geologic time ends and the next begins. Therefore, the divisions of the geologic time scale depend on events in the history of life on Earth. **Figure 2** shows the major divisions of the geologic time scale.

Precambrian Time Geologic time begins with a long span of time called Precambrian Time (pree KAM bree un). Precambrian Time, which covers about 88 percent of Earth's history, ended 542 million years ago. Few fossils survive from this time period.

Eras Geologists divide the time between Precambrian Time and the present into three long units of time called **eras.** They are the Paleozoic Era, the Mesozoic Era, and the Cenozoic Era.

Periods Eras are subdivided into units of geologic time called **periods.** You can see in **Figure 2** that the Mesozoic Era includes three periods: the Triassic Period, the Jurassic Period, and the Cretaceous Period.

The names of many of the geologic periods come from places around the world where geologists first described the rocks and fossils of that period. For example, the name *Cambrian* refers to Cambria, a Latin name for Wales. The rocks shown below are in Wales. The dark bottom layer dates from the Cambrian period.

apply it!

Refer to the geologic time scale shown in **Figure 2** to answer the questions below.

Suppose you want to make a model of the geologic time scale. You decide to use a scale of 1 cm = 1 million years.

1 Not counting Precambrian time, which era would take up the most space? _____

2 **Make Models** How long would the Mesozoic Era be in your model? _____

3 CHALLENGE Suppose you used a different scale: 1 m = 1 million years. What would be one advantage and one disadvantage of this scale?

_____
_____
_____
_____
_____
_____

 Do the Quick Lab *Going Back in Time.*

Assess Your Understanding

1a. Define The geologic time scale is a record of _____ and _____.

b. Sequence Number the following periods in order from earliest to latest.

Neogene _____ Jurassic _____
Quaternary _____ Triassic _____
Cretaceous _____

c. Draw Conclusions Refer to My Planet Diary and **Figure 2**. During which period did modern humans arise?

_____

got it? ....

○ I get it! Now I know that geologic time _____
_____

○ I need extra help with _____

Go to MY SCIENCE COACH online for help with this subject.

Early Earth

🔑 **How Did Earth Form?**

my planet Diary

Exploring Life Under Water

Dr. Anna-Louise Reysenbach always loved water sports. She was also interested in organisms that live in strange, extreme environments. Now, as a biology professor at Portland State University in Oregon, she gets to combine her two loves—and learn about early life on Earth!

Dr. Reysenbach uses submersibles, or submarines, to study bacteria that live deep under the ocean. No sunlight reaches these depths. There, hot water carrying dissolved minerals from inside Earth flows out through vents. Some kinds of bacteria use chemical energy from this material to make food, much as plants use the energy from sunlight. Scientists think that these bacteria are very similar to some of the earliest forms of life on Earth.

CAREERS

✏️ **Communicate** Discuss the work of Dr. Reysenbach with a partner. Then answer these questions on your own.

1. How are the bacteria near ocean vents different from many other organisms on Earth?

_____

_____

_____

2. Would you like to work under water in a submersible? Why, or why not?

_____

_____

_____

_____

> **PLANET DIARY** Go to **Planet Diary** to learn more about deep ocean vents.

Lab zone® Do the Inquiry Warm-Up *How Could Planet Earth Form in Space?*

Vocabulary
• comet

Skills
🔁 Reading: Sequence
△ Inquiry: Communicate

How Did Earth Form?

Using radioactive dating, scientists have determined that the oldest rocks ever found on Earth are about 4 billion years old. But scientists think Earth formed even earlier than that.

The Age of Earth According to these scientists' hypothesis, the moon formed from material knocked loose when a very young Earth collided with another object. This means Earth and the moon are about the same age. Scientists have used radioactive dating to find the age of moon rocks that astronauts brought back to Earth. The oldest moon rocks are about 4.6 billion years old. Scientists infer that Earth is also roughly 4.6 billion years old—only a little older than those moon rocks.

Earth Takes Shape 🔁 **Scientists think that Earth began as a ball of dust, rock, and ice in space. Gravity pulled this mass together.** As Earth grew larger, its gravity increased, pulling in more dust, rock, and ice nearby.

The energy from collisions with these materials raised Earth's temperature until the planet was very hot. Scientists think that Earth may have become so hot that it melted. Denser materials sank toward the center, forming Earth's dense, iron core. Less dense, molten material hardened over time to form Earth's outer layers—the solid crust and mantle.

FIGURE 1 ·······················

Early Earth
This artist's illustration shows Earth shortly after the moon formed. Earth was hot and volcanic, and contained no liquid water. The moon was much closer to Earth than it is today. Over time, Earth's surface began to cool, forming solid land.

✎ **Make Generalizations**
Could life have existed on Earth at the time shown in the illustration? Why, or why not?

_____
_____
_____
_____

FIGURE 2 ....

Development of the Atmosphere

The illustration shows the difference between Earth's first and second atmospheres.

✎ **Relate Text and Visuals**
Fill in the missing information for each atmosphere.

First atmosphere
Gases included:

_____

Blown away by:

_____

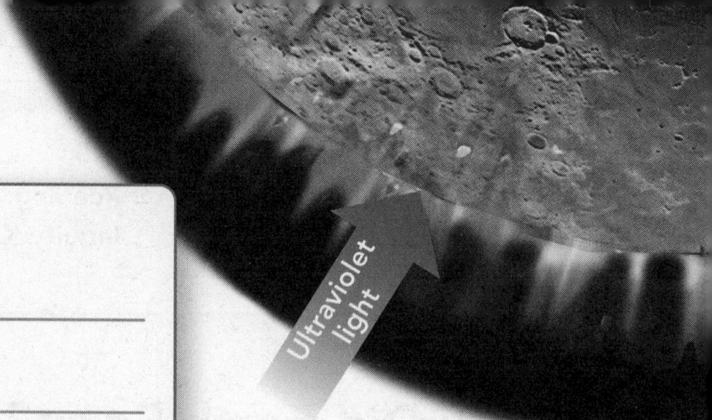

🌀 **Sequence** How did Earth's oceans develop over time?

1. _____
   _____
   _____

2. _____
   _____
   _____

3. _____
   _____
   _____

The Atmosphere Early Earth may have included light gases such as hydrogen and helium. Then the sun released strong bursts of particles called the solar wind. Earth's gravity could not hold the light gases, and the solar wind blew away Earth's first atmosphere.

After Earth lost its first atmosphere, a second atmosphere formed. Volcanic eruptions and collisions with comets added carbon dioxide, water vapor, nitrogen, and other gases to the atmosphere. A **comet** is a ball of dust, gas, and ice that orbits the sun. **Figure 2** shows the first and second atmospheres.

The Oceans At first, Earth's surface was too hot for water to remain a liquid. All water remained as water vapor. As Earth's surface cooled, the water vapor began to condense to form rain. The rainwater gradually accumulated and formed oceans. The oceans absorbed much of the carbon dioxide from the atmosphere.

The Continents During early Precambrian Time, much of Earth's rock cooled and hardened. Less than 500 million years after Earth formed, the rock at the surface formed continents.

Scientists have found that the continents move very slowly over Earth's surface because of forces inside Earth. Over billions of years, Earth's landmasses have repeatedly formed, broken apart, and then crashed together again.

Ultraviolet light

apply it!

❶ Draw a diagram showing Earth's structure after oceans began to form.

❷ **Communicate** Write a caption for your diagram explaining how Earth changed over time.

_____

_____

_____

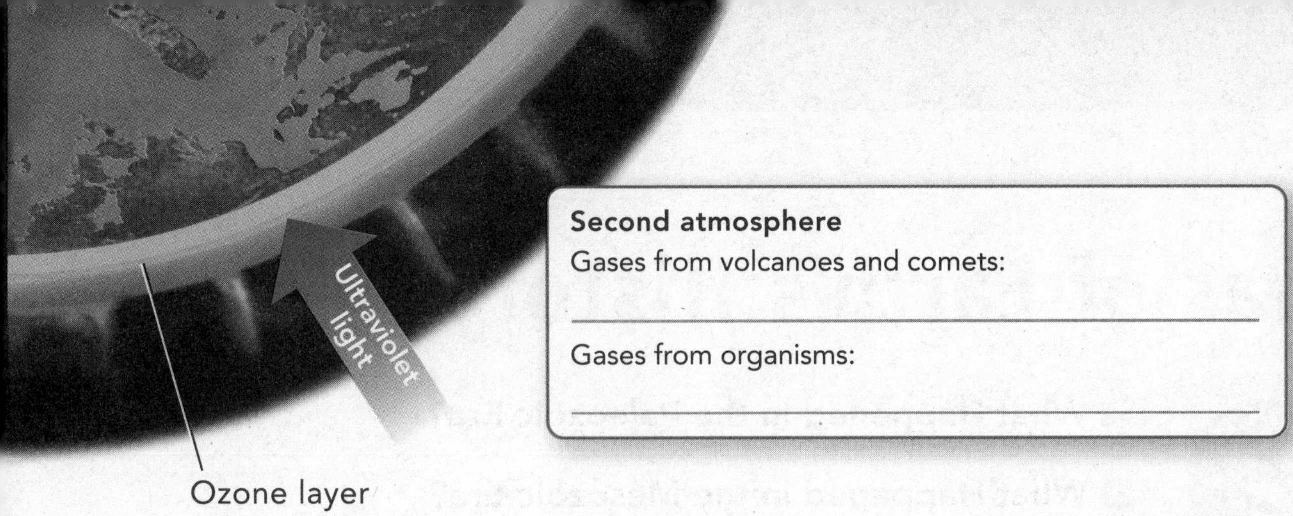

Ultraviolet light

Ozone layer

Second atmosphere
Gases from volcanoes and comets:

_____

Gases from organisms:

_____

Early Organisms

Scientists cannot pinpoint when or where life began on Earth. But scientists have found fossils of single-celled organisms in rocks that formed about 3.5 billion years ago. Scientists think that all other forms of life on Earth arose from these simple organisms. **Figure 3** shows remains of organisms similar to these early life forms. The bacteria Dr. Reysenbach studies are probably similar to these early organisms.

About 2.5 billion years ago, many organisms began using energy from the sun to make food. This process is called photosynthesis. One waste product of photosynthesis is oxygen. As organisms released oxygen, the amount of oxygen in the atmosphere slowly grew. Some oxygen changed into a form called ozone. The atmosphere developed an ozone layer that blocked the ultraviolet rays of the sun. Shielded from these rays, organisms could live on land.

FIGURE 3 ···
Stromatolites
These stromatolite fossils (stroh MAT uh lyt) from Australia are the remains of reefs built by early organisms. Some similar fossils are more than three billion years old.

Assess Your Understanding

1a. Identify Earth formed _____ years ago.

b. 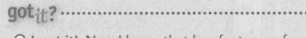 **Sequence** Write the numbers 1, 2, and 3 to show the correct order of the events below.

_____ Ozone layer forms.

_____ Earth loses its first atmosphere.

_____ Volcanoes and collisions with comets add water vapor to the atmosphere.

c. CHALLENGE How would Earth's atmosphere be different if organisms capable of photosynthesis had not evolved?

_____

_____

got it? ··

○ **I get it!** Now I know that key features of early Earth were _____

_____

_____

_____

_____

○ **I need extra help with** _____

Go to MY SCIENCE ⬥ COACH online for help with this subject.

127

Eras of Earth's History

🔑 **What Happened in the Paleozoic Era?**

🔑 **What Happened in the Mesozoic Era?**

🔑 **What Happened in the Cenozoic Era?**

my PLANET DiARY

FUN FACT

Mystery Metal

The rock layers in the photo hold evidence in one of the great mysteries of science: What killed the dinosaurs?

Find the thin, pale layer of rock marked by the ruler. This layer formed at the end of the Cretaceous period. It contains unusually high amounts of the metal iridium. At first, scientists could not explain the amount of iridium in this layer.

Iridium is more common in asteroids than on Earth. Many scientists now infer that an asteroid struck Earth. The impact threw dust into the air, blocking sunlight for years. About half the plant and animal species on Earth—including the dinosaurs—died out.

Think about what you know about fossils and Earth's history as you answer these questions.

1. What have many scientists inferred from the iridium found at the Cretaceous boundary?

_____

_____

_____

2. What are some questions you have about the history of life on Earth?

_____

_____

_____

> PLANET DIARY Go to **Planet Diary** to learn more about mass extinctions.

Lab zone® Do the Inquiry Warm-Up *Dividing History.*

Vocabulary
- invertebrate • vertebrate
- amphibian • reptile
- mass extinction • mammal

Skills
↻ **Reading:** Identify Supporting Evidence
△ **Inquiry:** Classify

What Happened in the Paleozoic Era?

The extinction of the dinosaurs is one of the most famous events in Earth's history, but it is just one example of the changes that have taken place. Through most of Earth's history, the only living things were single-celled organisms.

Near the end of Precambrian time, more complex living things evolved. Feathery, plantlike organisms anchored themselves to the seafloor. Jellyfish-like organisms floated in the oceans. Scientists have found fossils of such organisms in Australia, Russia, China, and southern Africa. But a much greater variety of living things evolved during the next phase of geologic time—the Paleozoic Era.

The Cambrian Explosion During the Cambrian Period, life took a big leap forward. ⚬ **At the beginning of the Paleozoic Era, a great number of different kinds of organisms evolved. For the first time, many organisms had hard parts, including shells and outer skeletons.** Paleontologists call this event the Cambrian Explosion because so many new life forms appeared within a relatively short time.

FIGURE 1 ·····································

Cambrian Life

The photo below shows a fossil of a Cambrian organism called *Anomalocaris*. The illustration shows one artist's idea of what *Anomalocaris* looked like.

✎ **Interpret Photos** What does the fossil tell you about what *Anomalocaris* looked like?

_____

_____

FIGURE 2

Changing Landscapes

✎ **Summarize** Based on the text and illustrations, describe the organisms in each period and how they differed from those in the previous period.

Silurian _____

_____

_____

_____

_____

_____

Invertebrates Develop At this time, all animals lived in the sea. Many were animals without backbones, or **invertebrates.** Invertebrates such as jellyfish, worms, and sponges made their home in the Cambrian ocean.

Brachiopods and trilobites were also common in the Cambrian seas. Brachiopods resembled modern clams, but are only distantly related to them. Trilobites were a huge and varied group of arthropods (AR thru pahds), animals with jointed legs and many body segments.

New Organisms Arise Invertebrates soon shared the seas with a new type of organism. During the Ordovician (awr duh VISH ee un) Period, the first vertebrates evolved. A **vertebrate** is an animal with a backbone. Jawless fishes with suckerlike mouths were the first vertebrates.

The First Land Plants Until the Silurian (sih LOOR ee un) Period, only one-celled organisms lived on the land. But during the Silurian Period, plants became abundant. These first, simple plants grew low to the ground in damp areas. By the Devonian Period (dih VOH nee un), plants that could grow in drier areas had evolved. Among these plants were the earliest ferns.

Early Fishes Both invertebrates and vertebrates lived in the Devonian seas. Even though the invertebrates were more numerous, the Devonian Period is often called the Age of Fishes. Every main group of fishes was present in the oceans at this time. Most fishes now had jaws, bony skeletons, and scales on their bodies. Sharks appeared in the late Devonian Period.

Silurian

Devonian

Animals Reach Land

The Devonian Period was also when animals began to spread widely on land. The first insects evolved during the Silurian Period, but vertebrates reached land during the Devonian. The first land vertebrates were lungfish with strong, muscular fins. The first amphibians evolved from these lungfish. An **amphibian** (am FIB ee un) is an animal that lives part of its life on land and part of its life in water.

The Carboniferous Period

Throughout the rest of the Paleozoic, other vertebrates evolved from amphibians. For example, small reptiles developed during the Carboniferous Period. **Reptiles** have scaly skin and lay eggs that have tough, leathery shells.

During the Carboniferous Period, winged insects evolved into many forms, including huge dragonflies and cockroaches. Giant ferns and cone-bearing plants formed vast swampy forests called coal forests. The remains of the coal-forest plants formed thick deposits of sediment that changed into coal over hundreds of millions of years.

Identify Supporting Evidence Underline the evidence that supports the statement, "The Devonian Period was also when animals began to spread widely on land."

Devonian _____

Carboniferous _____

Carboniferous

131

What two effects did the formation of Pangaea have?

_____

_____

_____

_____

Pangaea

During the Permian Period, between 299 and 250 million years ago, Earth's continents moved together to form a great landmass, or supercontinent, called Pangaea (pan JEE uh). The formation of Pangaea caused deserts to expand in the tropics. At the same time, sheets of ice covered land closer to the South Pole.

Mass Extinction

At the end of the Permian Period, most species of life on Earth died out. This was a **mass extinction,** in which many types of living things became extinct at the same time. Scientists estimate that about 90 percent of all ocean species died out. So did about 70 percent of species on land. Even widespread organisms like trilobites became extinct.

Scientists aren't sure what caused this extinction. Some think an asteroid struck Earth, creating huge dust clouds. Massive volcanic eruptions spewed carbon dioxide and sulfur dioxide into the atmosphere. Temperatures all over Earth rose during this time, too. The amount of carbon dioxide in the oceans increased and the amount of oxygen declined, though scientists aren't sure why. All these factors may have contributed to the mass extinction.

FIGURE 3 ⋯⋯⋯⋯⋯⋯⋯⋯⋯⋯⋯⋯⋯⋯⋯⋯⋯

Permian Trilobite

Throughout the Paleozoic, trilobites such as this Permian example were one of the most successful groups of organisms. But no species of trilobites survived the Permian mass extinction.

 Do the Quick Lab
Graphing the Fossil Record.

Assess Your Understanding

1a. List What are the periods of the Paleozoic Era?

_____

_____

_____

b. Sequence Number the following organisms in order from earliest to latest appearance.

amphibians _____ jawless fishes _____

trilobites _____ bony fishes _____

c. Relate Cause and Effect Name two possible causes of the mass extinction at the end of the Paleozoic.

_____

_____

_____

_____

_____

_____

got it? ⋯⋯⋯⋯⋯⋯⋯⋯⋯⋯⋯⋯⋯⋯⋯⋯⋯⋯⋯⋯⋯⋯⋯⋯⋯⋯⋯⋯⋯⋯

○ **I get it!** Now I know that the main events in the Paleozoic Era were _____

_____

○ I need extra help with _____

Go to MY SCIENCE ⓢ COACH online for help with this subject.

What Happened in the Mesozoic Era?

When you think of prehistoric life, do you think of dinosaurs? If so, you're thinking of the Mesozoic Era.

The Triassic Period Some living things managed to survive the Permian mass extinction. Plants and animals that survived included fish, insects, reptiles, and cone-bearing plants called conifers. 🔑 **Reptiles were so successful during the Mesozoic Era that this time is often called the Age of Reptiles.** The first dinosaurs appeared about 225 million years ago, during the Triassic (tri AS ik) Period.

Mammals also first appeared during the Triassic Period. A **mammal** is a vertebrate that can control its body temperature and feeds milk to its young. Mammals in the Triassic Period were very small, about the size of a mouse.

The Jurassic Period During the Jurassic Period (joo RAS ik), dinosaurs became common on land. Other kinds of reptiles evolved to live in the ocean and in the air. Scientists have identified several hundred different kinds of dinosaurs.

One of the first birds, called *Archaeopteryx,* appeared during the Jurassic Period. The name *Archaeopteryx* means "ancient winged one." Many paleontologists now think that birds evolved from dinosaurs.

apply it!

The illustrations show a flying reptile called *Dimorphodon* and one of the earliest birds, *Archaeopteryx.*

1 Identify two features the two animals have in common.

_____

_____

2 Identify one major difference between the two animals.

_____

_____

3 Classify Which animal is *Archaeopteryx*? How do you know it is related to birds?

_____

_____

133

FIGURE 4 ·····························

The End of the Dinosaurs

Many scientists hypothesize that an asteroid hit Earth near the present-day Yucatán Peninsula, in southeastern Mexico.

✎ CHALLENGE Write a short story summarizing the events shown in the illustration.

_____

_____

_____

_____

_____

_____

_____

_____

_____

The Cretaceous Period Reptiles, including dinosaurs, were still widespread throughout the Cretaceous Period (krih TAY shus). Birds began to replace flying reptiles during this period. Their hollow bones made them better adapted to their environment than the flying reptiles, which became extinct.

Flowering plants first evolved during the Cretaceous. Unlike conifers, flowering plants produce seeds that are inside a fruit. The fruit helps the seeds spread.

Another Mass Extinction 🔑 **At the close of the Cretaceous Period, about 65 million years ago, another mass extinction occurred. Scientists hypothesize that this mass extinction occurred when an asteroid from space struck Earth.** This mass extinction wiped out more than half of all plant and animal groups, including the dinosaurs.

When the asteroid hit Earth, the impact threw huge amounts of dust and water vapor into the atmosphere. Dust and heavy clouds blocked sunlight around the world for years. Without sunlight, plants died, and plant-eating animals starved. The dust later formed the iridium-rich rock layer you read about at the beginning of the lesson. Some scientists think that climate changes caused by increased volcanic activity also helped cause the mass extinction.

THE DEATH OF THE DINOSAURS
BY TERRY DACTYL

Lab® zone Do the Quick Lab
Modeling an Asteroid Impact.

🔑 Assess Your Understanding

got it? ···

○ **I get it!** Now I know that the main developments in the Mesozoic Era were _____

_____

○ **I need extra help with** _____

Go to MY SCIENCE ⓢ COACH online for help with this subject.

What Happened in the Cenozoic Era?

During the Mesozoic Era, mammals had to compete with dinosaurs for food and places to live. **The extinction of dinosaurs created an opportunity for mammals. During the Cenozoic Era, mammals evolved to live in many different environments—on land, in water, and even in the air.**

The Paleogene and Neogene Periods During the Paleogene and Neogene periods, Earth's climates were generally warm and mild, though they generally cooled over time. In the oceans, mammals such as whales and dolphins evolved. On land, flowering plants, insects, and mammals flourished. Grasses first began to spread widely. Some mammals became very large, as did some birds.

The Quaternary Period Earth's climate cooled and warmed in cycles during the Quaternary Period, causing a series of ice ages. Thick glaciers covered parts of Europe and North America. The latest warm period began between 10,000 and 20,000 years ago. Over thousands of years, most of the glaciers melted.

In the oceans, algae, coral, mollusks, fish, and mammals thrived. Insects and birds shared the skies. Flowering plants and mammals such as bats, cats, dogs, cattle, and humans became common. The fossil record suggests that modern humans may have evolved as early as 190,000 years ago. By about 12,000 to 15,000 years ago, humans had migrated to every continent except Antarctica.

FIGURE 5 ···

Giant Mammals

Many giant mammals evolved in the Cenozoic Era. This *Megatherium* is related to the modern sloth shown to the right, but was up to six meters tall.

✎ **Measure About how many times taller was *Megatherium* than a modern sloth?** _____

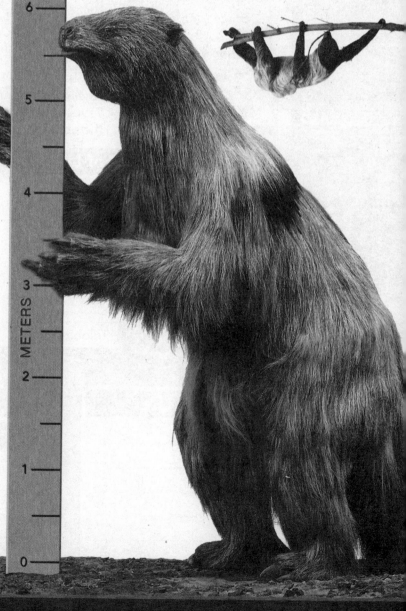

Geologic History

> ART IN MOTION **How do scientists study Earth's past?**

FIGURE 6 ··
This timeline shows key events in Earth's history. Use what you have learned to fill in the missing information.

ERA	▶ Precambrian Time	Paleozoic		
MILLIONS OF YEARS AGO	**4,600**	**542**	**488**	**444**

PERIOD

Geologic Events

Precambrian Time
- Earth forms about 4.6 billion years ago.
- Oceans form and cover Earth about 4 billion years ago.
- First sedimentary rocks form more than 3.8 billion years ago.

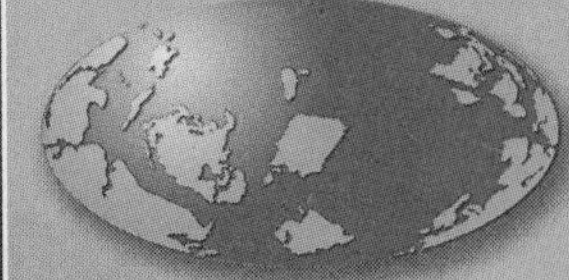

▶ CAMBRIAN
- Shallow seas cover much of the land.
- Ancient continents lie near or south of the equator.

▶ ORDOVICIAN
- Warm, shallow seas cover much of Earth.
- Ice cap covers what is now North Africa.

▶ SILURIAN
- Coral reefs develop.
- Early continents collide with what is now North America, forming mountains.

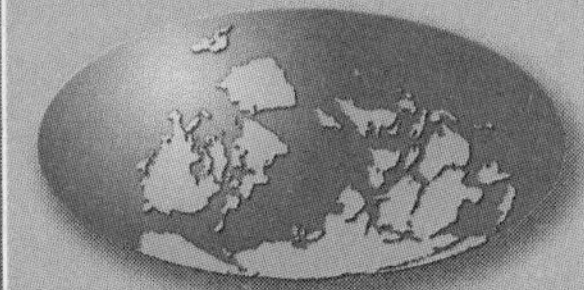

Early plant

Development of Life
_____
_____
_____
_____

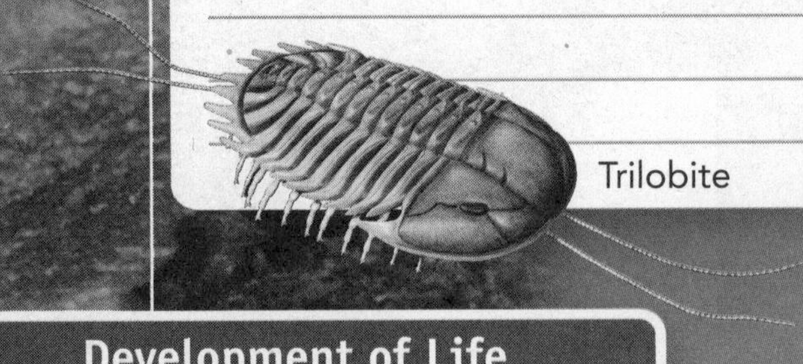

Trilobite

Development of Life
_____
_____
_____
_____

Sea scorpion

Development of Life
_____
_____
_____
_____

Sea pen

Development of Life
_____
_____
_____

Ammonite

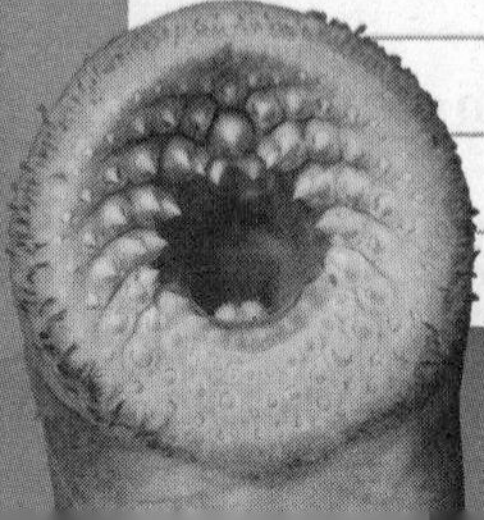

Jawless fish

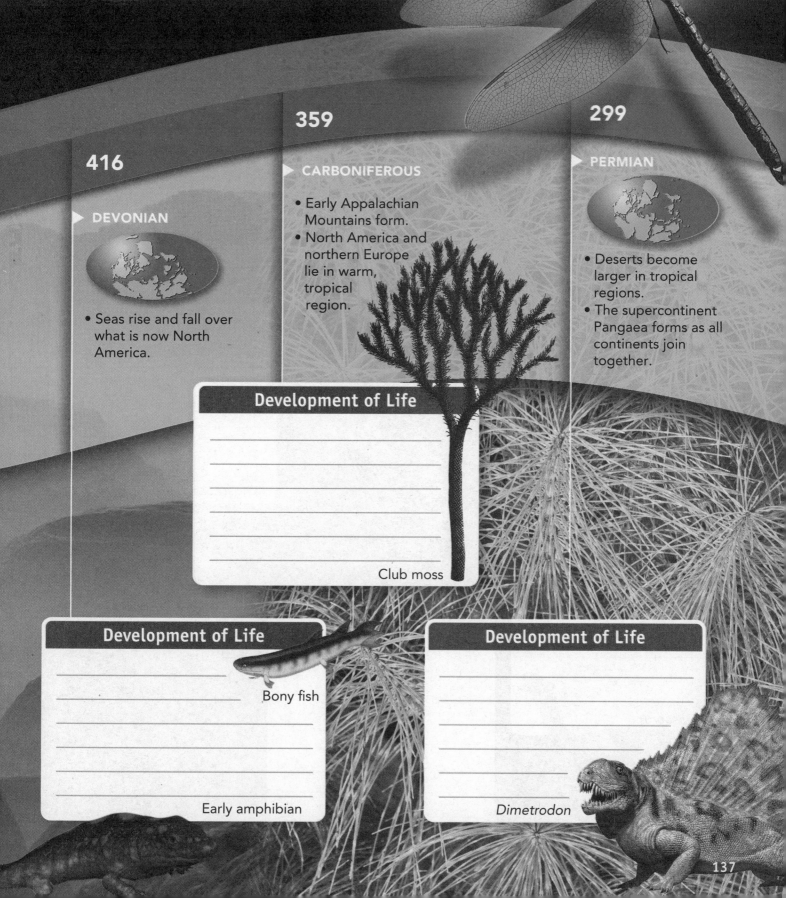

Note: To make the timeline easier to read, periods are shown at the about the same size, though some were longer than others. They are not drawn to scale.

Giant dragonfly (Carboniferous)

359

416

▶ **CARBONIFEROUS**

- Early Appalachian Mountains form.
- North America and northern Europe lie in warm, tropical region.

299

▶ **PERMIAN**

- Deserts become larger in tropical regions.
- The supercontinent Pangaea forms as all continents join together.

▶ **DEVONIAN**

- Seas rise and fall over what is now North America.

Development of Life

Club moss

Development of Life

Bony fish

Early amphibian

Development of Life

Dimetrodon

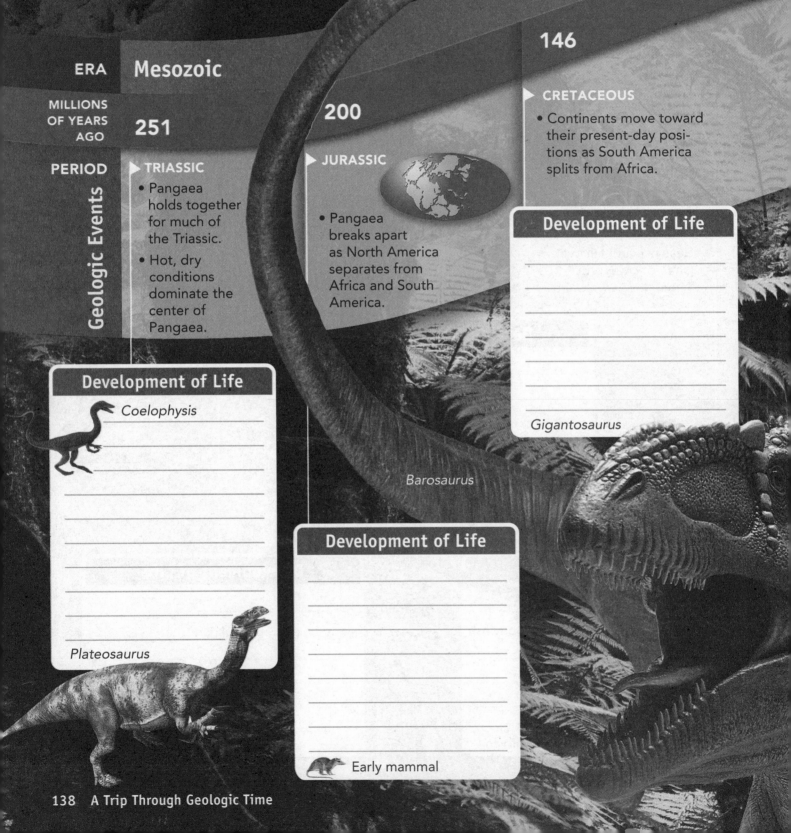

Geologic History

ERA	Mesozoic		
MILLIONS OF YEARS AGO	251	200	146
PERIOD	▶ TRIASSIC	▶ JURASSIC	▶ CRETACEOUS

Geologic Events

TRIASSIC
- Pangaea holds together for much of the Triassic.
- Hot, dry conditions dominate the center of Pangaea.

JURASSIC
- Pangaea breaks apart as North America separates from Africa and South America.

CRETACEOUS
- Continents move toward their present-day positions as South America splits from Africa.

Development of Life

Coelophysis

Plateosaurus

Development of Life

Early mammal

Barosaurus

Development of Life

Gigantosaurus

Cenozoic

66

▶ **PALEOGENE**

- Australia becomes a separate continent.
- Heavy volcanic activity occurs in the Pacific and Atlantic Oceans.

23

▶ **NEOGENE**

- Climates change frequently, generally becoming drier.
- Grasslands spread.
- The Andes and Himalayas form.
- North and South America are connected.

1.8

▶ **QUATERNARY**

- Thick glaciers advance and retreat over much of North America and Europe, parts of South America and Asia, and all of Antarctica.

Development of Life

Bat

Hyracotherium

Development of Life

Early hominid

Titanis (giant bird)

Development of Life

Woolly mammoth

Lab zone® Do the Quick Lab _Cenozoic Timeline._

🔑 Assess Your Understanding

2a. **Identify** (Grasses/Flowering plants) first spread widely in the Cenozoic Era.

b. **Explain** What factors allowed new organisms to spread during the Cenozoic Era?

_____
_____
_____
_____

c. **ANSWER THE BIG ?** How do scientists study Earth's past? Use an example from this chapter in your answer.

_____
_____
_____
_____
_____

got it? ....

○ **I get it!** Now I know that important events in the Cenozoic Era included _____
_____

○ **I need extra help with** _____

Go to **MY SCIENCE⑤ COACH** online for help with this subject.

Scientists study _____ in order to draw inferences about how _____ have changed over time.

LESSON 1 Fossils

🔑 Most fossils form when sediment hardens into rock, preserving the shapes of organisms.

🔑 Fossils include molds, casts, petrified fossils, carbon films, trace fossils, and preserved remains.

🔑 Fossils provide evidence about Earth's history.

Vocabulary
- fossil • mold • cast • petrified fossil
- carbon film • trace fossil • paleontologist
- evolution • extinct

LESSON 2 The Relative Age of Rocks

🔑 In horizontal sedimentary rock layers, the oldest layer is generally at the bottom. Each layer is younger than the layers below it.

🔑 Gaps in the geologic record and folding can change the position in which rock layers appear.

Vocabulary
- relative age • absolute age
- law of superposition • extrusion • intrusion
- fault • index fossil • unconformity

LESSON 3 Radioactive Dating

🔑 During radioactive decay, the atoms of one element break down to form atoms of another element.

🔑 In radioactive dating, scientists compare the amount of a radioactive element in a rock with the amount of the stable element into which the radioactive element decays.

Vocabulary
- radioactive decay
- half-life

LESSON 4 The Geologic Time Scale

🔑 Because the time span of Earth's past is so great, geologists use the geologic time scale to show Earth's history.

Vocabulary
- geologic time scale
- era
- period

LESSON 5 Early Earth

🔑 Scientists think that Earth began as a ball of dust, rock, and ice in space. Gravity pulled this mass together.

Vocabulary
- comet

LESSON 6 Eras of Earth's History

🔑 During the Paleozoic Era, a great number of different organisms evolved.

🔑 Reptiles spread widely during the Mesozoic Era.

🔑 During the Cenozoic Era, mammals evolved to live in many different environments.

Vocabulary
- invertebrate • vertebrate • amphibian • reptile
- mass extinction • mammal

Review and Assessment

LESSON 1 Fossils

1. A hollow area in sediment in the shape of all or part of an organism is called a

a. mold.   b. cast.

c. trace fossil.   d. carbon film.

2. A series of dinosaur footprints in rock are an example of a(n) _____ fossil.

3. Develop Hypotheses Which organism has a better chance of leaving a fossil: a jellyfish or a bony fish? Explain.

_____

_____

_____

Use the picture below to answer Questions 4–5.

4. Classify What type of fossil is shown?

_____

5. Infer This fossil was found in a dry, mountainous area. What can you infer about how the area has changed over time?

_____

_____

_____

6. Write About It Suppose you are developing a museum exhibit about fossils. Write a guide for visitors to your exhibit explaining how fossils form and what scientists can learn from them.

LESSON 2 The Relative Age of Rocks

7. A gap in the geologic record that occurs when sedimentary rocks cover an eroded surface is called a(n)

a. intrusion.   b. unconformity.

c. fault.   d. extrusion.

8. A geologist finds an area of undisturbed sedimentary rock. The _____ layer is most likely the oldest.

9. Apply Concepts A geologist finds identical index fossils in a rock layer in the Grand Canyon in Arizona and in a rock layer in northern Utah, more than 675 kilometers away. What can she infer about the ages of the two rock layers?

_____

_____

LESSON 3 Radioactive Dating

10. The time it takes for half of a radioactive element's atoms to decay is its

a. era.   b. half-life.

c. relative age.   d. absolute age.

11. Calculate The half-life of carbon-14 is 5,730 years. A basket has 25% of its carbon-14 remaining. About how old is the basket?

_____

12. Solve Problems Uranium-235 has a half-life of 713 million years. Would uranium-235 or carbon-14 be more useful for dating a fossil from Precambrian time? Explain.

_____

_____

_____

LESSON 4 **The Geologic Time Scale**

13. The geologic time scale is subdivided into

    a. relative ages.   **b.** absolute ages.

    c. unconformities.   **d.** eras and periods.

14. Scientists developed the geologic time scale by studying _____

_____

15. **Sequence** Which major division of geologic time came first?

_____

Which period of geologic time occurred most recently?

_____

LESSON 5 **Early Earth**

16. Which of the following was found in Earth's first atmosphere?

    a. carbon dioxide   **b.** hydrogen

    c. oxygen   **d.** ozone

17. Over time, Earth's rock hardened and formed land called _____

18. **Explain** How do scientists think that Earth's oceans formed?

_____

_____

_____

19. 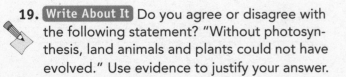 **Write About It** Do you agree or disagree with the following statement? "Without photosynthesis, land animals and plants could not have evolved." Use evidence to justify your answer.

LESSON 6 **Eras of Earth's History**

20. The earliest multicelled organisms were

    a. invertebrates.   **b.** land plants.

    c. vertebrates.   **d.** bacteria.

21. **Explain** How did Earth's environments change from the Neogene to the Quaternary Period?

_____

_____

22. **Evaluate Science in the Media** If you see a movie in which early humans fight dinosaurs, how would you judge the scientific accuracy of that movie? Give reasons for your judgment.

_____

_____

_____

_____

_____

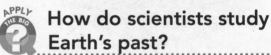

How do scientists study Earth's past?

23. Look at the fossil below. What can you infer about the organism and its environment? Be sure to give evidence for your inferences.

_____

_____

_____

_____

_____

_____

_____

Standardized Test Prep

Multiple Choice

Circle the letter of the correct answer.

1. Use the table to answer the question.

Geologic Time Scale	
Time Period	**Duration (Millions of Years)**
Cenozoic Era	66
Mesozoic Era	185
Paleozoic Era	291
Precambrian Time	about 4,058

A class is designing an outdoor model to show the geologic time scale from Precambrian Time through the present. If they use a scale of 1 m = 100 million years, how long will their model be?

A 46,000 m   **B** 460 m

C 46 m   **D** 4.6 m

2. A leaf falls into a shallow lake and is rapidly buried in the sediment. The sediment changes to rock over millions of years. Which type of fossil would **most likely** be formed?

A carbon film

B cast

C preserved remains

D trace fossil

3. What change in Earth's atmosphere allowed organisms to live on land?

A a collision with a comet

B the development of the ozone layer

C a strong burst of particles from the sun

D the absorption of carbon dioxide by oceans

4. Which of the following organisms lived during the Paleozoic Era?

A dinosaurs

B flowering plants

C grasses

D trilobites

5. Scientists can determine the absolute age of rocks using

A fault lines.

B index fossils.

C radioactive dating.

D the law of superposition.

Constructed Response

Use the diagram below and your knowledge of science to answer Question 6. Write your answer on a separate sheet of paper.

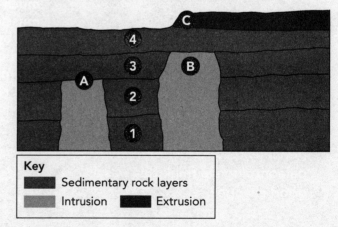

Key	
Sedimentary rock layers	
Intrusion	Extrusion

6. Write the order in which the rock areas shown formed. Justify your answer using evidence from the diagram.

PUTTING THE PUZZLE TOGETHER

Imagine you are putting together a puzzle, but you don't have all the pieces. That's the problem for scientists trying to determine exactly what an animal looked like. Paleontologists may find only some of the bones of a prehistoric animal. They may find bones from more than one of the same kind of animal.

Scientists build reconstructions of the animals based on the fossils they have and observations of living relatives of the animal. Computed tomography (CT) scans help scientists make virtual fossils. They start with the pieces they have and then fill in the rest of the puzzle virtually. For example, if the scientists have found a fossil of the right jaw bone, the computers are able to help them model the left jaw bone, and build virtual models of the entire head.

Bones tell a story that scientists can understand. It's much harder to figure out the size and shape of the muscles or the color of the animal. Different scientists will build slightly different reconstructions of the same kind of animal. Because so many pieces of the puzzle are missing, it may be impossible to have a perfectly accurate reconstruction. Because the organisms are extinct, scientists may never know for sure.

Write About It Research the different ways in which paleontologists have reconstructed *Tyrannosaurus rex*. Choose one change and explain how it differed from a previous reconstruction. Why did paleontologists think this was a good change?

These scientists are studying a Messel snake fossil on a digital scanning system. ▶

Teen Finds Fossils

In early 2007, sixteen-year-old Sierra Sarti-Sweeney went for a walk at Boca Ciega Millenium Park in Seminole, Florida. She wanted to take some nature pictures. She did not expect to stumble on a mammoth!

During her walk, Sierra noticed bones in a stream bed. With her older brother, Sean, she brought the bones to local scientists. The bone Sierra found was the tooth of a prehistoric Columbian mammoth. Archaeologists say that the tooth and other fossils Sierra found could be as much as 100,000 years old!

Since Sierra's find, digging at the site has uncovered even more bones, including those from prehistoric camels, 2-meter turtles, and saber-toothed cats. According to scientists, the findings suggest that this part of Florida was once like the African savanna region.

For Sierra, the experience was exciting. She even had a call from a late-night television host. Finding the tooth confirmed Sierra's desire to be a zoologist and to keep looking at the world around her.

Design It Plan an exhibit of Sierra's findings. What would people want to know and see? Make a brochure advertising your exhibit and develop a presentation of the fossils found at Boca Ciega Millenium Park.

FROZEN EVIDENCE

In the giant ice cap at the South Pole, a continuous record of snow exists reaching back more than 800,000 years. Scientists have drilled 3.2 kilometers down into the ice. From the cores they pull up, scientists learn about the temperature and the different gases in the air when each layer was formed.

These cores show that temperatures go up and down in cycles. Long ice ages (about 90,000 years) follow short warm periods (about 10,000 years). The climate record also shows that temperatures and amounts of carbon dioxide change together. If carbon dioxide levels rise, temperatures also rise.

Research It Find at least three sources that explain the ice cores project. Write an essay critiquing the explanations provided. Note any bias, misinformation, or missing information.

Researchers extract samples from the ice at the South Pole. ▲

APPENDIX A

Safety Symbols

These symbols warn of possible dangers in the laboratory and remind you to work carefully.

 Safety Goggles Wear safety goggles to protect your eyes in any activity involving chemicals, flames or heating, or glassware.

 Lab Apron Wear a laboratory apron to protect your skin and clothing from damage.

 Breakage Handle breakable materials, such as glassware, with care. Do not touch broken glassware.

 Heat-Resistant Gloves Use an oven mitt or other hand protection when handling hot materials such as hot plates or hot glassware.

 Plastic Gloves Wear disposable plastic gloves when working with harmful chemicals and organisms. Keep your hands away from your face, and dispose of the gloves according to your teacher's instructions.

 Heating Use a clamp or tongs to pick up hot glassware. Do not touch hot objects with your bare hands.

 Flames Before you work with flames, tie back loose hair and clothing. Follow instructions from your teacher about lighting and extinguishing flames.

 No Flames When using flammable materials, make sure there are no flames, sparks, or other exposed heat sources present.

 Corrosive Chemical Avoid getting acid or other corrosive chemicals on your skin or clothing or in your eyes. Do not inhale the vapors. Wash your hands after the activity.

 Poison Do not let any poisonous chemical come into contact with your skin, and do not inhale its vapors. Wash your hands when you are finished with the activity.

 Fumes Work in a well-ventilated area when harmful vapors may be involved. Avoid inhaling vapors directly. Only test an odor when directed to do so by your teacher, and use a wafting motion to direct the vapor toward your nose.

 Sharp Object Scissors, scalpels, knives, needles, pins, and tacks can cut your skin. Always direct a sharp edge or point away from yourself and others.

 Animal Safety Treat live or preserved animals or animal parts with care to avoid harming the animals or yourself. Wash your hands when you are finished with the activity.

 Plant Safety Handle plants only as directed by your teacher. If you are allergic to certain plants, tell your teacher; do not do an activity involving those plants. Avoid touching harmful plants such as poison ivy. Wash your hands when you are finished with the activity.

 Electric Shock To avoid electric shock, never use electrical equipment around water, or when the equipment is wet or your hands are wet. Be sure cords are untangled and cannot trip anyone. Unplug equipment not in use.

 Physical Safety When an experiment involves physical activity, avoid injuring yourself or others. Alert your teacher if there is any reason you should not participate.

 Disposal Dispose of chemicals and other laboratory materials safely. Follow the instructions from your teacher.

 Hand Washing Wash your hands thoroughly when finished with an activity. Use soap and warm water. Rinse well.

 General Safety Awareness When this symbol appears, follow the instructions provided. When you are asked to develop your own procedure in a lab, have your teacher approve your plan before you go further.

Using a Laboratory Balance

The laboratory balance is an important tool in scientific investigations. You can use a balance to determine the masses of materials that you study or experiment with in the laboratory.

Different kinds of balances are used in the laboratory. One kind of balance is the triple-beam balance. The balance that you may use in your science class is probably similar to the balance illustrated in this Appendix. **To use the balance properly, you should learn the name, location, and function of each part of the balance you are using. What kind of balance do you have in your science class?**

The Triple-Beam Balance

The triple-beam balance is a single-pan balance with three beams calibrated in grams. The back, or 100-gram, beam is divided into ten units of 10 grams each. The middle, or 500-gram, beam is divided into five units of 100 grams each. The front, or 10-gram, beam is divided into ten units of 1 gram each. Each of the units on the front beam is further divided into units of 0.1 gram. What is the largest mass you could find with a triple-beam balance?

The following procedure can be used to find the mass of an object with a triple-beam balance:
1. Place the object on the pan.
2. Move the rider on the middle beam notch by notch until the horizontal pointer on the right drops below zero. Move the rider back one notch.
3. Move the rider on the back beam notch by notch until the pointer again drops below zero. Move the rider back one notch.
4. Slowly slide the rider along the front beam until the pointer stops at the zero point.
5. The mass of the object is equal to the sum of the readings on the three beams.

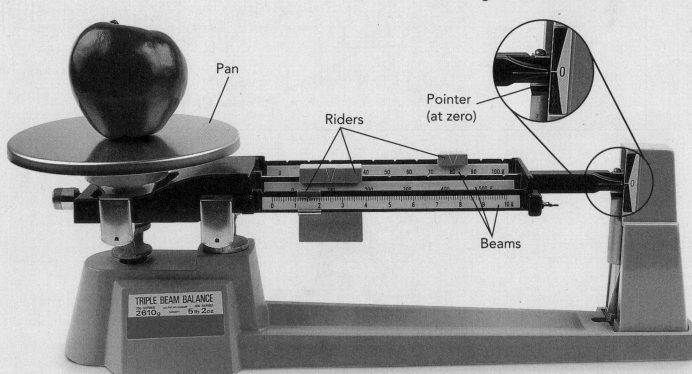

Pan

Riders

Pointer
(at zero)

Beams

TRIPLE BEAM BALANCE
700 SERIES   800 SERIES
2610g   CAPACITY 5 lb 2 oz

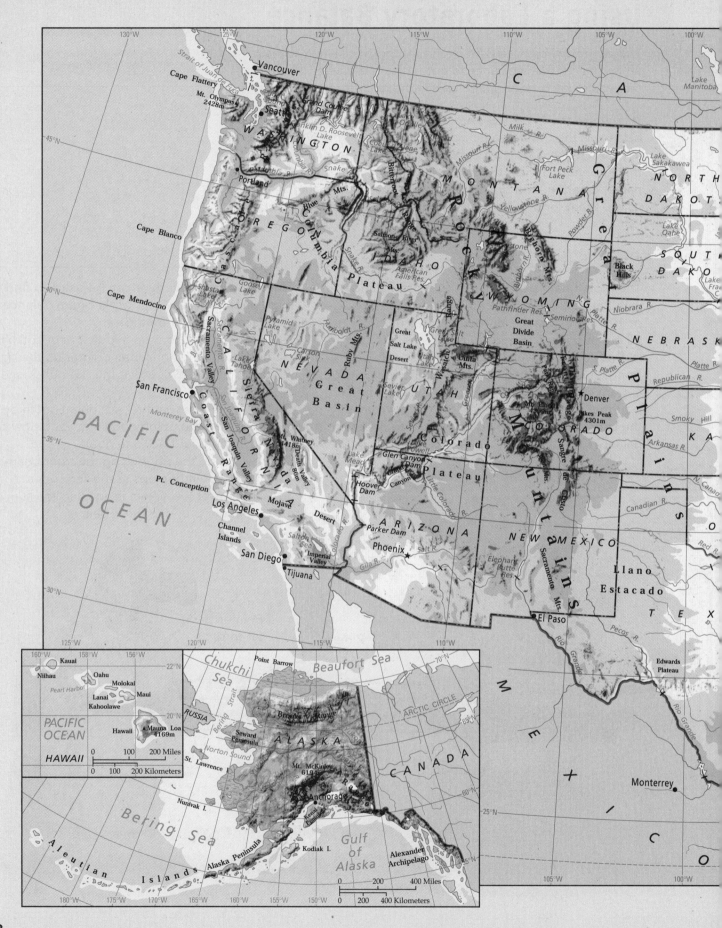

UNITED STATES
Physical

International boundary
State boundary
⊛ Washington, D.C.   National capital
★ Atlanta   State capital
● Detroit   Major city

ELEVATION

Meters		Feet
Over 3,000		Over 10,000
1,500 to 3,000		5,000 to 10,000
6,00 to 1,500		2,000 to 5,000
300 to 600		1,000 to 2,000
150 to 300		500 to 1,000
0 to 150		0 to 500
Below sea level		Below sea level

WATER DEPTH

Less than 200		Less than 600
Greater than 200		Greater than 600

0   100   200   300 Miles

0   100   200   300 Kilometers

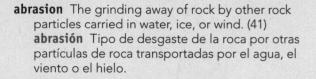

GLOSSARY

A

abrasion The grinding away of rock by other rock particles carried in water, ice, or wind. (41)
abrasión Tipo de desgaste de la roca por otras partículas de roca transportadas por el agua, el viento o el hielo.

absolute age The age of a rock given as the number of years since the rock formed. (111)
edad absoluta Edad de una roca basada en el número de años de su formación.

aerial photograph A photograph taken by cameras mounted in airplanes. (20)
fotografía aérea Fotografía tomada por cámaras instaladas en aviones.

alluvial fan A wide, sloping deposit of sediment formed where a stream leaves a mountain range. (76)
abanico aluvial Depósito de sedimento ancho e inclinado que se forma donde un arroyo sale de una cordillera.

amphibian A vertebrate whose body temperature is determined by the temperature of its environment, and that lives its early life in water and its adult life on land. (131)
anfibio Animal vertebrado cuya temperatura corporal depende de la temperatura de su entorno, y que vive la primera etapa de su vida en el agua y su vida adulta en la tierra.

B

beach Wave-washed sediment along a coast. (88)
playa Sedimento depositado por las olas a lo largo de una costa.

bedrock Rock that makes up Earth's crust; also the solid rock layer beneath the soil. (47)
lecho rocoso Roca que compone la corteza terrestre; también, la capa sólida de roca debajo del suelo.

C

carbon film A type of fossil consisting of an extremely thin coating of carbon on rock. (106)
película de carbono Tipo de fósil que consiste en una capa de carbono extremadamente fina que recubre la roca.

cast A fossil that is a solid copy of an organism's shape, formed when minerals seep into a mold. (106)
vaciado Fósil que es una copia sólida de la forma de un organismo y que se forma cuando los minerales se filtran y crean un molde.

chemical weathering The process that breaks down rock through chemical changes. (40)
desgaste químico Proceso que erosiona la roca mediante cambios químicos.

comet A loose collection of ice and dust that orbits the sun, typically in a long, narrow orbit. (126)
cometa Cuerpo poco denso de hielo y polvo que orbita alrededor del Sol. Generalmente su órbita es larga y estrecha.

conservation plowing Soil conservation method in which weeds and dead stalks from the previous year's crop are plowed into the ground. (55)
arado de conservación Método de conservación de la tierra en el que las plantas y los tallos muertos de la cosecha del año anterior se dejan en la tierra al ararla.

continental glacier A glacier that covers much of a continent or large island. (81)
glaciar continental Glaciar que cubre gran parte de un continente o una isla grande.

contour interval The difference in elevation from one contour line to the next. (25)
intervalo entre curvas de nivel Diferencia de elevación de una curva de nivel a la próxima.

contour line A line on a topographic map that connects points of equal elevation. (25)
curva de nivel Línea de un mapa topográfico que conecta puntos con la misma elevación.

contour plowing Plowing fields along the curves of a slope to prevent soil loss. (55)
arado en contorno Arar los campos siguiendo las curvas de una pendiente para evitar la pérdida del suelo.

crop rotation The planting of different crops in a field each year to maintain the soil's fertility. (55)
rotación de las cosechas Cultivo anual de cosechas diferentes en un campo para mantener la fertilidad del suelo.

D

decomposer An organism that gets energy by breaking down wastes and dead organisms, and returns raw materials to the soil and water. (50)
descomponedor Organismo que obtiene energía al descomponer desechos y organismos muertos y que devuelve la materia resultante al suelo y al agua.

deflation The process by which wind removes surface materials. (91)
deflación Proceso por el cual el viento se lleva materiales de la superficie.

degree A unit used to measure distances around a circle. One degree equals 1/360 of a full circle. (14)
grado Unidad usada para medir distancias alrededor de un círculo. Un grado es igual a 1/360 de un círculo completo.

delta A landform made of sediment that is deposited where a river flows into an ocean or lake. (76)
delta Accidente geográfico formado por sedimento que se deposita en la desembocadura de un río a un océano o lago.

deposition Process in which sediment is laid down in new locations. (67)
sedimentación Proceso por el cual los sedimentos se asientan en nuevos sitios.

digitizing Converting information to numbers for use by a computer. (19)
digitalizar Convertir información en números para que la use una computadora.

E

elevation Height above sea level. (4)
elevación Altura sobre el nivel del mar.

equator An imaginary line that circles Earth halfway between the North and South poles. (15)
ecuador Línea imaginaria que rodea la Tierra por el centro, equidistante de los polos norte y sur.

era One of the three long units of geologic time between the Precambrian and the present. (123)
era Cada una de las tres unidades largas del tiempo geológico entre el precámbrico y el presente.

erosion The process by which water, ice, wind, or gravity moves weathered particles of rock and soil. (39, 66)
erosión Proceso por el cual el agua, el hielo, el viento o la gravedad desplazan partículas desgastadas de roca y suelo.

evolution Change over time; the process by which modern organisms have descended from ancient organisms. (109)
evolución Cambios a través del tiempo; proceso mediante el cual los organismos modernos han descendido de los organismos antiguos.

extinct 1. Term used to refer to a group of related organisms that has died out and has no living members. (109) **2.** Term used to describe a volcano that is no longer active and unlikely to erupt again.
extinto 1. Término que se refiere a un grupo de organismos que ha muerto y no tiene miembros vivos. **2.** Término que describe un volcán que ya no es activo y es poco probable que haga erupción otra vez.

extrusion An igneous rock layer formed when lava flows onto Earth's surface and hardens. (112)
extrusión Capa de roca ígnea formada cuando la lava fluye hacia la superficie de la Tierra y se endurece.

F

fault A break in Earth's crust along which rocks move. (112)
falla Fisura en la corteza terrestre a lo largo de la cual se desplazan las rocas.

fertility A measure of how well soil supports plant growth. (48)
fertilidad Medida de cuán apropiado es un suelo para estimular el crecimiento de las plantas.

flood plain The flat, wide area of land along a river. (74)
llanura de aluvión Área de tierra extensa y plana a lo largo de un río.

fossil Preserved remains or traces of an organism that lived in the past. (105)
fósil Restos o vestigios conservados de un organismo que vivió en el pasado.

frost wedging Process that splits rock when water seeps into cracks, then freezes and expands. (41)
acuñado rocoso Proceso que separa las rocas cuando el agua se filtra entre grietas y luego se congela y expande.

GLOSSARY

G

Geographic Information System A system of computer hardware and software used to produce interactive maps. (22)
Sistema de Información Geográfica Sistema de equipos y programas computarizados que se usa para producir mapas interactivos.

geologic time scale A record of the geologic events and life forms in Earth's history. (121)
escala de tiempo geológico Registro de los sucesos geológicos y de las formas de vida en la historia de la Tierra.

glacier Any large mass of ice that moves slowly over land. (81)
glaciar Cualquier masa grande de hielo que se desplaza lentamente sobre la tierra.

Global Positioning System A navigation system that uses satellite signals to locate a radio receiver on Earth's surface. (22)
sistema de posicionamiento global Sistema de navegación que usa señales satelitales para ubicar un receptor de radio en la superficie de la Tierra.

globe A sphere that represents Earth's entire surface. (11)
globo terráqueo Esfera que representa toda la superficie de la Tierra.

gravity The attractive force between objects; the force that moves objects downhill. (68)
gravedad Fuerza que atrae a los cuerpos entre sí; fuerza que mueve un cuerpo cuesta abajo.

groundwater Water that fills the cracks and spaces in underground soil and rock layers. (78)
aguas freáticas Agua que llena las grietas y huecos de las capas subterráneas de tierra y roca.

gully A large channel in soil that carries runoff after a rainstorm. (72)
barranco Canal grande en el suelo formado por corrientes de agua durante una tormenta de lluvia.

H

half-life The time it takes for half of the atoms of a radioactive element to decay. (117)
vida media Tiempo que toma descomponer la mitad de los átomos de un elemento radiactivo.

headland A part of the shore that sticks out into the ocean. (87)
promontorio Parte de la costa que se interna en el mar.

hemisphere One half of the sphere that makes up Earth's surface. (15)
hemisferio Mitad de la esfera que forma la superficie de la Tierra.

humus Dark-colored organic material in soil. (47)
humus Material orgánico de color oscuro del suelo.

I

ice age Time in Earth's history during which glaciers covered large parts of the surface. (81)
edad de hielo Período en la historia de la Tierra durante el cual gran parte de la superficie terrestre estaba cubierta por glaciares.

index contour On a topographic map, a heavier contour line that is labeled with elevation of that contour line. (25)
curva de nivel índice En un mapa topográfico, curva de nivel más gruesa que lleva rotulada la elevación de esa curva de nivel.

index fossil Fossils of widely distributed organisms that lived during a geologically short period. (113)
fósil guía Fósiles de organismos altamente dispersos que vivieron durante un período geológico corto.

intrusion An igneous rock layer formed when magma hardens beneath Earth's surface. (112)
intrusión Capa de roca ígnea formada cuando el magma se endurece bajo la superficie de la Tierra.

invertebrate An animal without a backbone. (130)
invertebrado Animal sin columna vertebral.

K

karst topography A region in which a layer of limestone close to the surface creates deep valleys, caverns, and sinkholes. (79)
topografía kárstica Región en la que una capa de piedra caliza cerca de la superficie crea valles hundidos, grutas y pozos.

kettle A small depression that forms when a chunk of ice is left in glacial till. (84)
marmita glacial Pequeña depresión formada cuando un trozo de hielo se asienta en arcilla glacial.

key A list of the symbols used on a map and their meanings. (12)
clave Lista de los símbolos de un mapa y sus significados.

---------------- **L** ----------------

landform A feature of topography formed by the processes that shape Earth's surface. (5)
accidente geográfico Característica de la topografía creada por los procesos de formación de la superficie de la Tierra.

landform region A large area of land where the topography is made up mainly of one type of landform. (8)
región con accidentes geográficos Terreno amplio donde la topografía está compuesta, principalmente, por un tipo de accidente geográfico.

latitude The distance in degrees north or south of the equator. (16)
latitud Distancia en grados al norte o al sur del ecuador.

law of superposition The geologic principle that states that in horizontal layers of sedimentary rock, each layer is older than the layer above it and younger than the layer below it. (111)
ley de la superposición Principio geológico que enuncia que, en las capas horizontales de las rocas sedimentarias, cada capa es más vieja que la capa superior y más joven que la capa inferior.

loam Rich, fertile soil that is made up of about equal parts of clay, sand, and silt. (48)
marga Suelo rico y fértil formado por partes casi iguales de arcilla, arena y limo.

loess A wind-formed deposit made of fine particles of clay and silt. (92)
loes Depósito de partículas finas de arcilla y limo arrastradas por el viento.

longitude The distance in degrees east or west of the prime meridian. (17)
longitud Distancia en grados al este o al oeste del meridiano cero.

longshore drift The movement of water and sediment down a beach caused by waves coming in to shore at an angle. (88)
deriva litoral Movimiento de agua y sedimentos paralelo a una playa debido a la llegada de olas inclinadas respecto a la costa.

---------------- **M** ----------------

mammal A vertebrate whose body temperature is regulated by its internal heat, and that has skin covered with hair or fur and glands that produce milk to feed its young. (133)
mamífero Vertebrado cuya temperatura corporal es regulada por su calor interno, cuya piel está cubierta de pelo o pelaje y que tiene glándulas que producen leche para alimentar a sus crías.

map A flat model of all or part of Earth's surface as seen from above. (11)
mapa Modelo plano de toda la superficie de la Tierra o parte de ella tal y cómo se ve desde arriba.

map projection A framework of lines that helps to transfer points on Earth's surface onto a flat map. (11)
proyección de mapa Esquema de líneas que facilita la transferencia de puntos de la superficie terrestre a un mapa plano.

mass extinction When many types of living things become extinct at the same time. (132)
extinción en masa Situación que ocurre cuando muchos tipos de seres vivos se extinguen al mismo tiempo.

mass movement Any one of several processes by which gravity moves sediment downhill. (68)
movimiento en masa Cualquiera de los procesos por los cuales la gravedad desplaza sedimentos cuesta abajo.

meander A looplike bend in the course of a river. (75)
meandro Curva muy pronunciada en el curso de un río.

mechanical weathering The type of weathering in which rock is physically broken into smaller pieces. (40)
desgaste mecánico Tipo de desgaste en el cual una roca se rompe físicamente en trozos más pequeños.

mold A type of fossil that is a hollow area in sediment in the shape of an organism or part of an organism. (106)
molde Tipo de fósil que consiste en una depresión del sedimento que tiene la forma de un organismo o de parte de un organismo.

moraine A ridge formed by the till deposited at the edge of a glacier. (84)
morrena Montículo formado por arcilla glaciárica depositada en el borde de un glaciar.

mountain A landform with high elevation and high relief. (7)
montaña Accidente geográfico con una elevación alta y un relieve alto.

GLOSSARY

mountain range A group of mountains that are closely related in shape, structure, area, and age. (7)
cordillera Grupo de montañas que están estrechamente relacionadas en forma, estructura y edad.

_____ N _____

natural resource Anything naturally occurring in the environment that humans use. (53)
recurso natural Cualquier elemento generado naturalmente en el medio ambiente y que los humanos usan.

_____ O _____

oxbow lake A meander cut off from a river. (75)
lago de recodo Meandro que ha quedado aislado de un río.

oxidation A chemical change in which a substance combines with oxygen, as when iron oxidizes, forming rust. (43)
oxidación Cambio químico en el cual una sustancia se combina con el oxígeno, como cuando el hierro se oxida, y produce herrumbre.

_____ P _____

paleontologist A scientist who studies fossils to learn about organisms that lived long ago. (108)
paleontólogo Científico que estudia fósiles para aprender acerca de los organismos que vivieron hace mucho tiempo.

period One of the units of geologic time into which geologists divide eras. (123)
período Una de las unidades del tiempo geológico en las que los geólogos dividen las eras.

permeable Characteristic of a material that contains connected air spaces, or pores, that water can seep through easily. (44)
permeable Característica de un material que contiene diminutos espacios de aire, o poros, conectados por donde se puede filtrar el agua.

petrified fossil A fossil in which minerals replace all or part of an organism. (106)
fósil petrificado Fósil en el cual los minerales reemplazan todo el organismo o parte de él.

pH scale A range of values used to indicate how acidic or basic a substance is; expresses the concentration of hydrogen ions in a solution. (48)
escala de pH Rango de valores que se usan para indicar el grado acídico o básico de una sustancia; expresa la concentración de los iones de hidrógeno de una solución.

pixel One bit of a digitized image, often appearing as a small square or dot. (19)
pixel Trozo pequeño de una imagen digital que a menudo aparece como un cuadrado o punto pequeño.

plain A landform made up of flat or gently rolling land with low relief. (6)
llanura Accidente geográfico que consiste en un terreno plano o ligeramente ondulado con un relieve bajo.

plateau A large landform that has high elevation and a more or less level surface. (7)
meseta Accidente geográfico que tiene una elevación alta y cuya superficie es más o menos nivelada.

plucking The process by which a glacier picks up rocks as it flows over the land. (83)
extracción Proceso por el cual un glaciar arranca las rocas al fluir sobre la tierra.

prime meridian The line that makes a half circle from the North Pole to the South Pole and that passes through Greenwich, England. (15)
meridiano cero Línea que forma un medio círculo desde el polo norte al polo sur y que pasa por Greenwich, Inglaterra.

_____ R _____

radioactive decay The process in which the nuclei of radioactive elements break down, releasing fast-moving particles and energy. (117)
desintegración radiactiva Proceso de descomposición del núcleo de los elementos radiactivos que libera partículas en movimiento y energía.

relative age The age of a rock compared to the ages of other rocks. (110)
edad relativa Edad de una roca comparada con la edad de otras rocas.

relief The difference in elevation between the highest and lowest parts of an area. (5)
relieve Diferencia de elevación entre las partes más altas y más bajas de un área.

reptile A vertebrate whose temperature is determined by the temperature of its environment, that has lungs and scaly skin, and that lays eggs on land. (131)
  reptil Animal vertebrado cuya temperatura depende de la temperatura de su entorno, que tiene pulmones, piel con escamas y que pone huevos en la tierra.

rill A tiny groove in soil made by flowing water. (72)
  arroyo Pequeño surco en el suelo causado por el paso del agua.

runoff Water that flows over the ground surface rather than soaking into the ground. (71)
  escurrimiento Agua que fluye sobre la superficie en lugar de ser absorbida por el suelo.

S

sand dune A deposit of wind-blown sand. (92)
  duna de arena Depósito de arena arrastrada por el viento.

satellite image A picture of the land surface based on computer data collected from satellites. (20)
  imagen satelital Representación visual de la superficie terrestre basada en la colección de datos de un satélite.

scale Used to relate distance on a map or globe to distance on Earth's surface. (12)
  escala Se usa para relacionar la distancia de un mapa o globo terráqueo con la distancia de la superficie de la Tierra.

sediment Small, solid pieces of material that come from rocks or the remains of organisms; earth materials deposited by erosion. (67)
  sedimento Trozos pequeños y sólidos de materiales que provienen de las rocas o de los restos de organismos; materiales terrestres depositados por la erosión.

soil The loose, weathered material on Earth's surface in which plants can grow. (47)
  suelo Material suelto y desgastado de la superficie terrestre donde crecen las plantas.

soil conservation The management of soil to limit its destruction. (55)
  conservación del suelo Cuidado del suelo para limitar su destrucción.

soil horizon A layer of soil that differs in color and texture from the layers above or below it. (49)
  horizonte de suelo Capa de suelo de color y textura diferentes a las capas que tiene encima o abajo.

spit A beach formed by longshore drift that projects like a finger out into the water. (89)
  banco de arena Playa formada por la deriva litoral, que se proyecta como un dedo dentro del agua.

stalactite An icicle-like structure that hangs from the ceiling of a cavern. (78)
  estalactita Estructura en forma de carámbano que cuelga del techo de una caverna.

stalagmite A columnlike form that grows upward from the floor of a cavern. (78)
  estalagmita Estructura en forma de columna que crece hacia arriba desde el suelo de una caverna.

stream A channel through which water is continually flowing downhill. (72)
  riachuelo Canal por el cual el agua fluye continuamente cuesta abajo.

subsoil The layer of soil below topsoil that has less plant and animal matter than topsoil and contains mostly clay and other minerals. (49)
  subsuelo Capa de suelo debajo del suelo superior que tiene menos materia de plantas y animales que el suelo superior, y que principalmente contiene arcilla y otros minerales.

surveying The process of gathering data for a map by using instruments and the principles of geometry to determine distance and elevations. (19)
  agrimensura Proceso que consiste en reunir información para un mapa y en el cual se determinan distancias y elevaciones usando instrumentos y principios geométricos.

symbol On a map, a picture used by mapmakers to stand for features on Earth's surface. (12)
  símbolo En un mapa, imagen que usan los cartógrafos para representar los diferentes aspectos de la superficie de la Tierra.

T

till The sediments deposited directly by a glacier. (84)
  arcilla glaciárica Sedimentos depositados directamente por un glaciar.

topographic map A map that shows the surface features of an area. (25)
  mapa topográfico Mapa que muestra los accidentes geográficos de la superficie terrestre de un área.

topography The shape of the land determined by elevation, relief, and landforms. (4)
  topografía Forma del terreno determinada por la elevación, el relieve y los accidentes geográficos.

GLOSSARY

topsoil The crumbly, topmost layer of soil made up of clay and other minerals and humus (nutrients and decaying plant and animal matter). (49)
suelo superior Capa superior arenosa del suelo formada por arcilla, otros minerales y humus (nutrientes y materia orgánica de origen vegetal y animal).

trace fossil A type of fossil that provides evidence of the activities of ancient organisms. (107)
vestigios fósiles Tipo de fósil que presenta evidencia de las actividades de los organismos antiguos.

tributary A stream or river that flows into a larger river. (72)
afluente Río o arroyo que desemboca en un río más grande.

U

unconformity A gap in the geologic record that shows where rock layers have been lost due to erosion. (114)
discordancia Interrupción en el récord geológico que muestra dónde las capas rocosas se han perdido a causa de la erosión.

uniformitarianism The geologic principle that the same geologic processes that operate today operated in the past to change Earth's surface. (38)
uniformitarianismo Principio geológico que enuncia que los mismos procesos geológicos que cambian la superficie de la Tierra en la actualidad ocurrieron en el pasado.

V

valley glacier A long, narrow glacier that forms when snow and ice build up in a mountain valley. (82)
glaciar de valle Glaciar largo y estrecho que se forma por la acumulación de hielo y nieve en el valle de una montaña.

vertebrate An animal with a backbone. (130)
vertebrado Animal con columna vertebral.

W

weathering The chemical and physical processes that break down rock and other substances. (39)
desgaste Procesos químicos y físicos que erosionan la roca y descomponen otras sustancias.

INDEX

INDEX

INDEX

ACKNOWLEDGMENTS

Staff Credits

The people who made up the *Interactive Science* team—representing composition services, core design digital and multimedia production services, digital product development, editorial, editorial services, manufacturing, and production—are listed below.

Jan Van Aarsen, Samah Abadir, Ernie Albanese, Zareh MacPherson Artinian, Bridget Binstock, Suzanne Biron, MJ Black, Nancy Bolsover, Stacy Boyd, Jim Brady, Katherine Bryant, Michael Burstein, Pradeep Byram, Jessica Chase, Jonathan Cheney, Arthur Ciccone, Allison Cook–Bellistri, Rebecca Cottingham, AnnMarie Coyne, Bob Craton, Chris Deliee, Paul Delsignore, Michael Di Maria, Diane Dougherty, Kristen Ellis, Theresa Eugenio, Amanda Ferguson, Jorgensen Fernandez, Kathryn Fobert, Julia Gecha, Mark Geyer, Steve Gobbell, Paula Gogan–Porter, Jeffrey Gong, Sandra Graff, Adam Groffman, Lynette Haggard, Christian Henry, Karen Holtzman, Susan Hutchinson, Sharon Inglis, Marian Jones, Sumy Joy, Sheila Kanitsch, Courtenay Kelley, Chris Kennedy, Toby Klang, Greg Lam, Russ Lappa, Margaret LaRaia, Ben Leveillee, Thea Limpus, Dotti Marshall, Kathy Martin, Robyn Matzke, John McClure, Mary Beth McDaniel, Krista McDonald, Tim McDonald, Rich McMahon, Cara McNally, Melinda Medina, Angelina Mendez, Maria Milczarek, Claudi Mimo, Mike Napieralski, Deborah Nicholls, Dave Nichols, William Oppenheimer, Jodi O'Rourke, Ameer Padshah, Lorie Park, Celio Pedrosa, Jonathan Penyack, Linda Zust Reddy, Jennifer Reichlin, Stephen Rider, Charlene Rimsa, Stephanie Rogers, Marcy Rose, Rashid Ross, Anne Rowsey, Logan Schmidt, Amanda Seldera, Laurel Smith, Nancy Smith, Ted Smykal, Emily Soltanoff, Cindy Strowman, Dee Sunday, Barry Tomack, Patricia Valencia, Ana Sofia Villaveces, Stephanie Wallace, Christine Whitney, Brad Wiatr, Heidi Wilson, Heather Wright, Rachel Youdelman

Photography

All uncredited photos © 2011 Pearson Education.

Front Cover
Javarman/Shutterstock

Back Cover
Bryan Brazil/Shutterstock

Front Matter
Page ix, James L. Amos/Photo Researchers, Inc.; **vi,** Greg Epperson/Getty Images; **vii,** Kevin Schafer/Corbis; **viii,** Kushnirov Avraham/Fotolia; **xi laptop,** iStockphoto.com; **xiii girl,** JupiterImages/Getty Images; **xix inset,** John Cancalosi/Photo Researchers, Inc.; **xvi laptop,** iStockphoto.com; **xviii mountains inset,** Richard and Ellen Thane/Science Source; **xviii–xix bkgrnd,** Image Source/Getty Images.

Chapter 1
Pages xxii–1 spread, Greg Epperson/Getty Images; **3 t,** Corbis; **3 m2,** Charles O'Rear/Corbis; **3 b,** United States Geological Survey (USGS); **4 b,** Northwind Picture Archives/Alamy; **4 t,** Northwind Picture Archives/Alamy; **6 inset,** Wayne Barrett & Anne MacKay/Getty; **7 l inset,** DLILLC/Corbis; **7 r inset,** Ocean/Corbis; **8,** Angelo Cavalli/Corbis; **9 m1,** Anne W. Krause/Corbis; **9 m2,** Image Source/Getty Images; **9 b,** Wayne Barrett & Anne MacKay/Corbis; **9 t,** Egmont Strigl/Imagebroker/Alamy; **10–11 bkgrnd spread,** Frank Lukasseck/Getty Images; **18,** Zuma/Newscom; **19 l,** InterNetwork Media/Photodisc/Alamy; **19 r,** InterNetwork Media/Photodisc/Alamy; **20 l,** Charles O'Rear/Corbis; **20 r,** Charles O'Rear/Corbis; **21,** GeoEye/Photo Researchers, Inc.; **24,** Kai-Uwe Och/Alamy; **25 l,** Corbis; **25 r,** United States Geological Survey (USGS); **26,** United States Geological Survey (USGS); **28,** Wayne Barrett & Anne MacKay/Getty Images; **30,** United States Geological Survey (USGS).

Interchapter Feature
Page 32 bkgrnd, Gordon Wiltsie/Getty; **32 map inset,** Earthquake Hazards Program/United States Geological Survey (USGS); **33 b,** iStockphoto.com; **33 t,** JupiterImages/Comstock Images/Alamy.

Chapter 2
Pages 34–35, Corbis/Kevin Schafer; **37 t,** Susan Rayfield/Photo Researchers, Inc.; **37 m,** PhotoAlto/Alamy; **37 b,** Stockbyte/SuperStock; **38 inset,** NASA/JPL/AP Images; **38 bkgrnd,** NASA/JPL/Cornell University/ZUMA/Corbis; **39 b,** Timothy Hearsum/Getty Images; **39 t,** Adam Jones/Getty Images; **40 bkgrnd,** Alexander Benz/Corbis; **41 tr,** Fletcher & Baylis/Science Source; **41 bl,** Susan Rayfield/Photo Researchers, Inc.; **41 tl,** Tom Till/Getty Images; **41 m,** Travel Ink/Alamy; **41 br,** Jim Nicholson/Alamy; **41 bkgrnd,** Alexander Benz/Corbis; **42 t,** Bob Hammerstrom/The Nashua Telegraph/Newscom; **42 b,** Jim Cole/AP Images; **43 inset,** Adam Hart-Davis/Photo Researchers, Inc.; **43 bkgrnd,** John Elk III/Alamy; **45 r,** Nancy Smith/Pearson; **45 l,** Nancy Smith/Pearson; **45 bkgrnd,** Nancy Smith/Pearson; **46 b,** Vinicius Ramalho Tupinamba/iStockphoto.com; **46 m,** Dr. Jeremy Burgess/Photo Researchers, Inc.; **46 t,** Dr. Tony Brain/Photo Researchers, Inc.; **47 bkgrnd,** Micha Pawlitzki/Corbis; **47 inset,** Timurd/Dreamstime.com; **51,** Andrew Bordwin/Beateworks/Corbis; **52 inset,** Dustbowl Farm, Dalhart, Texas (June, 1938), Dorothea Lange/Corbis; **52 bkgrnd,** Margaret Bourke-White (1954)/Time & Life Pictures/Getty Images; **53,** Glen Allison/Getty Images; **54 r,** Dino Ferretti/ANSA/Corbis; **54 l,** PhotoAlto/Alamy; **55 b,** Stockbyte/SuperStock; **55 tl,** Westend61 GmbH/Alamy; **55 tr,** Dr. Jeremy Burgess/Photo Researchers, Inc.

Interchapter Feature
Page 60 m, Caryn Becker/Alamy; **60 bkgrnd,** Caryn Becker/Alamy; **61,** Bettmann/Corbis.

Chapter 3
Pages 62–63 spread, Kushnirov Avraham/Fotolia; **65 t,** Marli Miller; **65 m1,** Kim Walker/Robert Harding World Imagery/Alamy; **65 m2,** Chris Jaksa/age Fotostock; **65 b,** blickwinkel/Alamy; **66,** Rick Bowmer/AP Images; **68 b,** China Daily/Reuters; **68 t,** CNImaging/Photoshot/Newscom; **69 l,** Marli Miller; **69 r,** Paolo Gislimberti/Alamy; **70,** Enrique Aguirre/Photolibrary New York; **72,** Michael Just/age Fotostock; **73 all,** Gail Jankus/Photo Researchers, Inc.; **74 l,** Darwin Wiggett/age Fotostock; **74 br,** Kim Walker/Robert Harding World Imagery/Alamy; **74–75 t,** Roine Magnusson/age fotostock/Alamy; **75 b,** Aflo/Nature Picture Library; **76 t,** Marli Miller; **76 l,** JPL/NGA/NASA; **78 bkgrnd,** Michael J Thompson/Shutterstock; **78 inset,** Bernhard Edmaier/Science Photo Library/Photo Researchers, Inc.;

79, Igor Katayev/ITAR-TASS/Landov; **80 m inset,** Harold Lund/Getty; **80–81 bkgrnd,** Arctos Images/Alamy; **81,** Landsat Image Mosaic of Antarctica/USGS/NASA; **82,** Chris Jaksa/age fotostock; **83,** David Nunuk/age Fotostock; **85,** Adam Jones/Science Source; **86–87 bkgrnd,** Radius Images/Photolibrary New York; **90 bkgrnd,** Andrew McConnell/Robert Harding World Imagery/Corbis; **90 m,** Courtesy of Margaret Hiza Redsteer; **90–91 bkgrnd,** McConnell/Robert Harding World Imagery/Corbis; **92 l inset,** Patrick Poendl/Shutterstock; **92 r inset,** blickwinkel/Alamy; **92–93 bkgrnd,** Ermin Gutenberger/iStockphoto.com; **93 l inset,** Richard and Ellen Thane/Science Source; **93 r inset,** Skip Brown/Getty Images; **94 b,** Andrew McConnell/Robert Harding World Imagery/Corbis; **94 t,** Adam Jones/Science Source.

Interchapter Feature
Page 98, Tony Campbell/iStockphoto.com; **99 bkgrnd,** JPL/NASA; **99 inset,** JPL/NASA.

Chapter 4
Pages 100–101 spread, Sinclair Stammers/Science Source; **103 t,** James L. Amos/Photo Researchers, Inc.; **103 m1,** Michael Szoenyi/Photo Researchers, Inc.; **103 m2,** Dr. Marli Miller/Getty Images; **103 m2,** Bedrock Studios/Dorling Kindersley; **104,** Phil Martin/PhotoEdit Inc.; **104 boy,** Diane Diederich/iStockphoto.com; **105,** Stock Connection/Newscom; **106 fern fossils,** Charles R. Belinky/Photo Researchers, Inc.; **106 insect fossil,** Breck P. Kent; **106 dinosaur footprint,** Andy Selinger/Alamy; **107 b,** Charlie Ott/Science Source; **107 t,** James L. Amos/Photo Researchers, Inc.; **107 m,** Dave King/Courtesy of the National Museum of Wales/Dorling Kindersley; **108 l,** WaterFrame/Alamy; **108 r,** Newscom; **108 m,** John Cancalosi/age Fotostock/Photolibrary New York; **109,** Phil Schermeister/Corbis; **111,** Jeff Foott/Discovery Channel Images/Getty Images; **112 t,** Michael Szoenyi/Photo Researchers, Inc.; **112 b,** G. R. Roberts/Photo Researchers, Inc.; **115,** Dr. Marli Miller/Getty Images; **116,** Bettmann/CORBIS; **119,** Archaeological Society SAP/AP Images; **120 r bkgrnd,** Jeremy Walker/Science Photo Library/Photo Researchers; **120 l bkgrnd,** Gianni Tortoli/Photo Researchers, Inc.; **120 br,** Dave King/Dorling Kindersley; **120 t,** Gary Ombler/Robert L. Braun, modelmaker/Dorling Kindersley; **121,** James L. Amos/Corbis; **122 smilodon,** Colin Keates/Courtesy of the Natural History Museum, London/Dorling Kindersley; **122 velociraptor,** Gary Ombler/Luis Rey, Modelmaker/Dorling Kindersley; **122 wiwaxia,** Chase Studio/Photo Researchers, Inc.; **122 chart t,** Peter Johnson/Corbis; **122 chart m2,** Georgette Douwma/Science Source; **122 chart m1,** Jeremy Walker/Science Photo Library/Photo Researchers; **122 chart b,** Gianni Tortoli/Photo Researchers, Inc.; **123,** R. Dolton/Alamy; **124 bkgrnd,** National Oceanic and Atmospheric Administration (NOAA); **124 bl inset,** National Oceanic and Atmospheric Administration (NOAA); **124 br inset,** National Oceanic and Atmospheric Administration (NOAA); **127,** Georgette Douwma/Science Source; **128 inset,** Francois Gohier/Photo Researchers, Inc.; **128 bkgrnd,** Mark Garlick/Photo Researchers, Inc.; **129 l,** Alan Sirulnikoff/Photo Researchers, Inc.; **129 r,** Stocktrek Images, Inc./Alamy; **130,** David Fleetham/Alamy; **132,** Sinclair Stammers/Photo Researchers, Inc.; **133 t,** Gary Ombler/Robert L. Braun,

modelmaker/Dorling Kindersley; **133 b,** John Downs/Dorling Kindersley; **133 bkgrnd,** Jeremy Walker/Science Photo Library/Photo Researchers; **133 bkgrnd,** Jeremy Walker/Science Photo Library/Photo Researchers; **135 l,** Harry Taylor/Courtesy of the Natural History Museum, London/Dorling Kindersley; **135 r,** Jerry Young/Dorling Kindersley; **136 sea pen,** Chase Studio/Photo Researchers, Inc.; **136 trilobite,** Chase Studio/Photo Researchers, Inc.; **136 jawless fish,** Gary Meszaros/Alamy; **136 ammonite,** Colin Keates/Courtesy of the Natural History Museum, London/Dorling Kindersley; **136 early plant,** Patrice Rossi Calkin; **136 sea scorpion,** Publiphoto/Photo Researchers, Inc.; **136 lava,** Gianni Tortoli/Photo Researchers, Inc.; **137 bkgrnd,** Greg Vaughn/Alamy; **137 bony fish,** De Agostini/Getty Images; **137 early amphibian,** Walter Myers/Stocktrek Images, Inc./Alamy; **137 giant dragonfly,** Steve Gorton/Courtesy of Oxford University Museum of Natural History/Dorling Kindersley; **137 club moss,** Sheila Terry/Photo Researchers, Inc.; **137 dimetrodon,** Bedrock Studios/Dorling Kindersley; **138 coelophysis,** Gary Ombler/Gary Staab, modelmaker/Dorling Kindersley; **138 plateosaurus,** Bedrock Studios/Dorling Kindersley; **138 barosaurus,** Dave King/Jeremy Hunt at Centaur Studios, modelmaker/Dorling Kindersley; **138 early mammal,** Malcolm McGregor/Dorling Kindersley; **138 gigantosaurus,** Jon Hughes/Bedrock Studios/Dorling Kindersley; **138–139 bison bkgrnd,** Peter Johnson/Corbis; **138–139 forest bkgrnd,** Jeremy Walker/Science Photo Library/Photo Researchers; **139 hyracotherium,** Harry Taylor/Courtesy of the Natural History Museum, London/Dorling Kindersley; **139 bat,** Bedrock Studios/Dorling Kindersley; **139 titanis,** Jon Hughes/Bedrock Studios/Dorling Kindersley; **139 early hominid,** Javier Trueba/Madrid Scientific Films/Photo Researchers, Inc.; **139 woolly mammoth,** Dave King/Courtesy of the National Museum of Wales/Dorling Kindersley; **141,** Colin Keates/Dorling Kindersley; **142,** John Cancalosi/Photo Researchers, Inc.; **140 b,** Georgette Douwma/Science Source; **140 t,** Dave King/Dorling Kindersley.

Interchapter Feature
Page 144 t, Steppenwolf/Alamy, **144 b,** Jonathan Blair/Corbis; **145 b,** Morton Beebe/Corbis; **145 tr,** Colin Keates/Courtesy of the Natural History Museum, London/Dorling Kindersley; **145 t bkgrnd,** Russell Sadur/Dorling Kindersley; **145 b inset,** Nick Cobbing/Alamy; **145 tl,** Dorling Kindersley/Getty Images.

take note

this space is yours—great for drawing diagrams and making notes

this is your book

you can write in it

this is your book

you can write in it

this is your book

you can write in it

take note

this space is yours—great for drawing diagrams and making notes

this is your book

you can write in it

170

take note

this space is yours—great for drawing diagrams and making notes

this is your book

you can write in it